Thank you for your expressions and thoughts about how Hardwiring Excellence in Education can help us all be the best leaders. --- *Dr. Janet Pilcher*

Janet Pilcher is one of the most visionary improvement leaders in the field today. Her new book, *Hardwiring Excellence in Education*, covers all bases on how to lead an organization in a post-pandemic world. It is an easy read that offers practical and actionable advice on handling almost any situation as a leader. This book is one that I will continue to reference and read repeatedly in reflection on how I am performing as a leader. The evidence-based leadership practices aligned with the nine principles has changed my life! Every leader should read this book and share it with their team! Come join the army of improvement leaders assembling across the United States!

**- Dr. Ryan Carpenter**
*Superintendent*
Estacada School District, OR

The success of our community depends on how well we educate our students. Our leadership team and leaders have been and will continue to be key to position Ysleta Independent School District to achieve our mission. The tools and tactics in *Hardwiring Excellence in Education* provide valuable resources as we continue to develop YISD leaders. That includes, hearing from our families and employees about how well we are doing and providing the highest level of service to those we serve.



Superintendent
Ysleta Independent School District, TX
President of Texas Association of
Latino Administrators and Superintendents

*Hardwiring Excellence in Education* feels fresh and current yet drives home the important concepts which are constant in our workplace. Janet does a great job of providing examples throughout the book - so no matter where an organization is on their excellence journey, a leader can identify with the book content. Janet states, "The most successful leaders are those who lead with an improvement mindset." - No truer words are in this book. At a time when the world needs more leaders executing with an improvement approach, she helps us understand how to apply a leadership framework of evidence-based actions that have positive and impactful outcomes for our organizations.

**- Dr. Natalie Harder**
*President*
Coker University, SC

There are many leadership books that discuss "what" leaders should do to move their district from good to great. In *Hardwiring Excellence in Education,* Janet does a beautiful job of describing the "how" of the work through success stories of organizational partners across the United States. Great leaders are always working to build a continuous improvement infrastructure that will last long after they leave their leadership position. Turning the Nine Principles Framework described in this book into a habit will weave measurable processes into the fabric of an organization and leave a legacy of positive impact.

**- Nannette Johnston**
*Studer Education Leader Coach 2016 – 2022*
Kentucky Superintendent of the Year 2014

*Hardwiring Excellence in Education* is the epitome of a solid resource to keep organizational cultures honest and in real-time, facing the complexities of a changing environment. In this book, Dr. Pilcher does an excellent job outlining each of the nine principles for leaders to uniquely follow, while also self-assessing their realities to move from complacency to a place of greatness. More importantly, *Hardwiring Excellence in Education* provides the necessary narratives, actions, and conceptual examples for leaders to consider while shaping and operationalizing organizational excellence. This book is simply masterful!

**- Dr. Vincent June**
*Chancellor*
South Louisiana Community College, LA

*Hardwiring Excellence in Education* is an excellent resource for leaders to use as a tool to develop a leadership team. This book outlines each of nine principles for leaders to follow to "hardwire" behaviors that lead to organizational excellence. Each chapter explains the principle, provides action steps to move an organization forward, and concludes by providing an example of "what right looks like" in practice within educational organizations striving for excellence.

**- Dr. Jennifer Nebelsick Lowery**
*Superintendent*
Tea Area School District 41-5, SD

*Hardwiring Excellence in Education* is an important and timely book. These are challenging days for our educational systems and Janet gives thoughtful descriptions of values and principles that can support and strengthen them. She also offers clear and practical tools designed to build culture and leadership at every level. She skillfully applies her own expertise with tried and tested methods from workplace development to educational environments while keeping it very real by sharing her own personal experiences throughout. Every chapter underline Janet's intention of developing leadership in everyone by "putting people first"!

**- Dr. Kim MacQueen**
*Vice-President*
Innisfree Hotels

*Hardwiring Excellence in Education* shows how we can develop positive workplace cultures where teams feel empowered to solve problems rather than admire them. If your team is stuck in the "been there done that and it didn't work" loop, and they're struggling to achieve results, Janet provides a practical path forward with this guide. The tools and tactics in this book build consistent leadership practices that help us serve others at high levels.

**- Jon Malone**
*Regional Director and Chief Executive*
Northwestern Illinois Association, IL

As leaders, we want to create excellent organizations that impact lives and endure over time. Janet Pilcher provides a powerful blueprint in *Hardwiring Excellence in Education* to achieve continuous growth and meaningful impact. Each day brings challenges. Building coherence within our complex systems is hard work. I look at what I do, what we do, differently now because of the principles in this book. We are learning how to listen deeply, strengthen our capacity to lead, and align our collective efforts. I see a path forward through the complexity. Growing leaders with the mindset and skillset to improve builds confidence and practice. We show up as one team with intention to live our shared values. Our improvement skillset is scaffolding to our next level leaders. We now know how to pause to determine if our actions are creating the impact we intend. Janet gives us a platform for more than leader development. The tools and tactics in this book guide our organizations down a path to fulfill our purpose, achieve greater experiences for each child, and create a better tomorrow for our communities. I'm grateful to be a partner in this work outlined in the book.

**- Dr. Ed Manansala**
*County Superintendent of Schools*
El Dorado County Office of Education, CA

*Hardwiring Excellence in Education* is a timely account for all leaders as we reestablish practices transitioning from a pandemic. Distinguished executives, like Janet, understand that building capacity in your people positions the organization to sustain excellence long term. As a superintendent, I value the connection in the text between accountability and culture. Professional courage is necessary if the standard is not to be compromised. Meade County School chases a process for preparing our students for a quality life and I am reinvigorated with this resource to help our students achieve success for years to come.

**- Dr. Mark J. Martin**
*Superintendent*
Meade County School District, KY

*Hardwiring Excellence in Education* provides simple, great examples and actions of "Always Behaviors" which benefit leaders in their quest to provide a workplace where Service Excellence is what we do daily. As we embrace continuous improvement and work toward hardwiring excellence in our organizations, this book serves as a guide for leaders to follow. It gives us an opportunity to be of service to each other, our students and their families, and our community.

**- Sergio Mendoza**
*Superintendent*
Burton School District, CA

I love this book! When I started reading it, I couldn't put it down. It's readable, very conversational, and very real. Not only does Janet show positive results and actions of our partner organizations, but she also tells her own stories. Often these are stories of leadership lessons she has learned. She balances the partner stories with lessons learned from her own leadership experiences. It's a powerful way to teach the tools and tactics with examples and stories.

**- Dr. KK Owen**
*Studer Education Leader Coach*
Retired from the Escambia County School District FL,
Director of Professional Learning

*Hardwiring Excellence in Education* is a book that finally brings the "hard" skills (methods and tools) and "soft" skills (relationship-building) of continuous improvement together. Through concrete examples and practical advice drawn from her own deep personal leadership experience, Janet Pilcher provides a clear roadmap for leaders interested in building high-performing organizations with integrity, care and rigor.

**- Dr. Sandra Park**
*Co-founder, Improvement Collective*
National Faculty, Carnegie Foundation

High performing organizations have an executive leadership team which sets the tone for a culture of service excellence and continuous improvement and invests in the development of their middle management for crucial long-term success. Janet Pilcher clearly lays out The Nine Principles Framework with practical and actionable advice to guide committed organizations to move from good to great and great to greater. Originally developed for healthcare systems, the nine principles have now helped shape numerous educational institutions from K-12 to higher education across the country to apply evidence-based practices. Waukesha County government is honored to consider the Studer Education team at Huron Consulting our partner. This work has hardwired our culture of engagement and service excellence where teammates work with their head up and understand why their work makes a difference to the citizens and businesses who call us home.

**- Dale Shaver**
*Director and County Executive Cabinet Advisor*
Waukesha County, WI

*Hardwiring Excellence in Education* is truly motivational, and the *Nine Principles* outlined by Janet Pilcher are essential for all current and aspiring leaders. It provides clear, straightforward examples for embedding continuous improvement into any business culture. About ten years ago, I had the great honor of meeting Dr. Pilcher. She brought the *Nine Principles* to the School District of Menomonee Falls. The tools necessary, as outlined in *Hardwiring,* to implement the *Nine Principles* were not a "solution of the month" but became the way of doing business in our District.

The tools empowered our staff closest to the "problems" to safely try new solutions. Staff felt like they belonged. The more success they saw, the more they wanted to improve. "The flywheel was spinning!!" The tools became a way of life and continue today even after key staff retirements. *Hardwiring Excellence in Education* is a must read. I often recommend the Studer *Nine Principles* to friends and colleagues in various industries. It was an honor to read Janet's latest book!! Like her other works, I will reread, often!

**- Faith M. VanderHorst**

*Retired, President and Board Member*

School District of Menomonee Falls, WI

# HARDWIRING EXCELLENCE IN EDUCATION

## NINE PRINCIPLES FRAMEWORK

DR. JANET PILCHER

Copyright Information



Published by:
Huron Consulting Services, LLC
550 W. Van Buren Street
Chicago, IL 60607
Phone: 312-583-8700
www.huronconsultinggroup.com

ISBN: 979-8-9878129-0-7



Printed in the United States of America

# CONTENTS

# INTRODUCTION

## *Nine Principles® Framework*

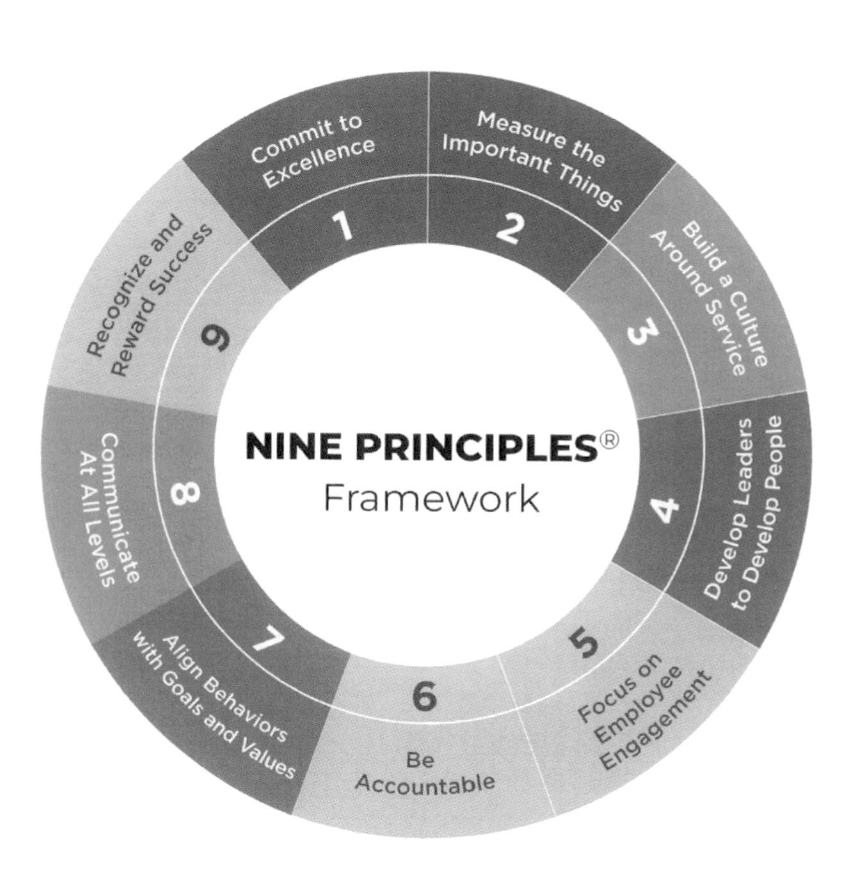

Educators are passionate people with a great purpose. We make a difference in the lives of those we serve. We offer students warm and safe places to belong and expand their thinking. We prepare students to be the solution builders of the future. Our work is important and worthwhile, and we are driven to make a difference in our students' lives.

I hope *Hardwiring Excellence in Education* reignites a flame to fuel your passion. I also hope that you open your hearts and minds to challenge your thinking about how we currently do our work. I've found that on average, educational organizations are good. In fact, when you ask leaders about their organizations, they rate them as good or very good. That's where we could face a dilemma. We believe what we do in our schools is good enough, which presents a challenge for us to improve and excel. However, we often find ourselves reacting to problems and feeling like we are constantly putting out fires.

During the time I am writing this book, our schools are facing significant teacher shortages. We don't have enough teachers or employees to staff our schools and districts. We feel frantic and our daily work feels chaotic. This is not a new problem; it's one that school leaders face throughout each school year. When we start the year understaffed, we do our work and the work of others because we are short-staffed. We feel stressed and take it out on those around us. We've simply reached our limit!

Eventually we hire enough teachers to staff our schools. When spring comes, the frantic cycle starts again. We focus time on recruiting teachers because of losing so many during or at the end of the school year.

Here's the challenge. We need more teachers and staff because we are losing more and more of them in our profession. Therefore, one of our most important goals is to create workplace environments that support and develop teachers and staff. When that occurs, our employees feel supported, and our students have greater opportunities to succeed.

To retain excellent teachers and staff, we need excellent leaders. Without excellent leaders, our educational systems can't move from good to great and great to greater. The challenge then, is how we take our success to the next level and improve where we have performance gaps. Leaders who create inspiring workplace environments and build strength in people take our educational systems to higher levels.

*Hardwiring Excellence in Education* is about leadership. ***It is for anyone who practices leadership regardless of their position in an organization.*** Our job is to be the very best. To be at our best, we constantly work on "getting better at getting better." The best coaches and teams never believe they are good enough. Every day they seek to build and sustain greatness. That's what great leaders do.

Since the inception of Studer Education, we've been fortunate to work alongside passionate and driven leaders at some of the best organizations. They are truly leaders in our field. Still, they want to get even better. Increasingly, I notice that it is most often the leaders at great organizations who are most committed to further improvement.

Those who succeed do so because their commitment flows for the right reasons: They want to provide the best education for students and the best workplace for employees.

It all starts with a commitment to **Purpose, Worthwhile Work, and Making a Difference**. These are the educational values that rest at the core of the excellence journey and the hub of the Organizational Flywheel referenced in this book. I've met many education professionals and nearly all of them say they are driven by these core values. That's why most of us became educators in the first place – and likely the reason why you are reading this book. The good always want to get better.

*Hardwiring Excellence in Education* includes many examples from the education profession. Some of you may work in other professions. The Nine Principles Framework described in this book can apply to you and your organization. As you read about the tools and tactics, think about how they translate into your work. The research that supports the Nine Principles Framework has an interdisciplinary focus on leadership excellence. At the end of this book, I've provided a current bibliography of sources used as we've developed the Nine Principles Framework tools and tactics.

The approaches and examples in *Hardwiring Excellence in Education* show how to execute leadership practices in ways that make them stick. That's what we mean by hardwiring – always applying actions that move us toward excellence.

The Nine Principles Framework (Figure 1) summarizes leadership beliefs to drive a continuous improvement culture. In *Hardwiring Excellence in Education*, I describe tools and tactics associated with each of the nine principles that build leadership skills to improve all aspects of our work. Continuous improvement is the backbone of an organizational excellence journey. The tools and tactics associated with the Nine Principles Framework support leadership behaviors that produce positive results.

| NINE PRINCIPLES FRAMEWORK | |
|---|---|
| **PRINCIPLE 1: COMMIT TO EXCELLENCE** | *Set high expectations to achieve results while living out mission and values.* |
| **PRINCIPLE 2: MEASURE THE IMPORTANT THINGS** | *Continuously track progress to achieve results with an improvement mindset.* |
| **PRINCIPLE 3: BUILD A CULTURE AROUND SERVICE** | *Serve others with great care and concern.* |
| **PRINCIPLE 4: DEVELOP LEADERS TO DEVELOP PEOPLE** | *Coach people to be their best at work.* |
| **PRINCIPLE 5: FOCUS ON EMPLOYEE ENGAGEMENT** | *Attend to aspirations and desires in the workplace.* |
| **PRINCIPLE 6: BE ACCOUNTABLE** | *Commit to individual accountability to achieve organizational goals.* |
| **PRINCIPLE 7: ALIGN BEHAVIORS WITH GOALS AND VALUES** | *Apply consistent practices to move the organization in a positive direction.* |
| **PRINCIPLE 8: COMMUNICATE AT ALL LEVELS** | *People know why what they do matters.* |
| **PRINCIPLE 9: REWARD AND RECOGNIZE SUCCESS** | *Value and appreciate people working together to get results.* |

*Figure 1. Nine Principles Framework*

In each chapter, I focus on tools and tactics associated with one of the nine principles. An Organizational Flywheel lays the groundwork for applying the Nine Principles Framework.

## The Organizational Flywheel

At the heart of the Organizational Flywheel (Figure 2) are the educational core values of **purpose, worthwhile work, and making a difference**. The values never change; they always stay the same. Those who commit to the values strengthen our profession. The other key parts of the flywheel are inspiring workplaces, building strength, and accelerating results.

*Figure 2. Organizational Excellence Flywheel*

Let's take a moment and reflect on what a flywheel does. A flywheel keeps a car's engine running; without a working flywheel, the engine would stall when we let off the accelerator. A flywheel balances the engine to run smoothly. The starter motor engages the starter ring on the edge of the flywheel to begin the rotation. The flywheel connects the engine transmission through a clutch to transfer power to the wheels. Without a working flywheel we would not be able to travel. As the flywheel spins faster and faster our speed increases. It takes a lot of energy to get the flywheel spinning. Without doing so we simply stall.

We can transfer this understanding of an engine flywheel to the Organizational Flywheel. Our purpose is to achieve and accelerate results which occur once the flywheel starts spinning. Holding true to our educational core values rests at the hub of the flywheel. We accelerate results by creating inspiring workplaces that give people opportunities to be at their best. We depend on our people to achieve success. When we develop and strengthen our people, our organization becomes stronger. The continued improvements and results spin the flywheel faster and faster.

Let's dig deeper into the parts of the flywheel – inspiring workplaces, building strength, and accelerating results.

### *Inspiring Workplaces*

We are lucky in education. Most of us are called to be part of the education profession because we are passionate about what we do. Regardless of the position, we are motivated to help students succeed.

In education, we are also trained to notice problems, focus on performance gaps, and react to failing systems. We are professionally trained to be problem identifiers. To a point this is good. We want to improve where we have gaps. However, constantly focusing on the negative shifts us away from having a positive culture. I'm not suggesting that we stop noticing what's wrong; the goal is to substantially increase our awareness of what's right and intentionally celebrate and accelerate those actions.

There is much to celebrate in education. We see wins occurring in our schools, departments, and classrooms every day. *Hardwiring Excellence in Education* focuses on tools and tactics we can apply to reinforce and celebrate areas working well. The tactics are critical to create the kind of organizational culture that spins the flywheel.

I recall an occurrence in my professional life that inspired me to be a good leader. When I was promoted from associate dean to dean of a college, a long-standing, highly respected faculty member who I admired wrote me a note and left it on my desk. When I returned to my office from a meeting, I sat in my chair, opened the note that read, "Sometimes the good guys win." The note ended with her signature. The meaning of the note has remained with me throughout my life. With that note, she inspired me to always strive to be at my best. Inspiring workplaces give people a chance to do their best work and to feel motivated to grow and develop their skills to do so. A simple, yet powerful note can make a huge difference.

Creating inspiring workplaces starts with building a culture of gratitude. People have an inherent desire to feel valued by others. When leaders show gratitude employees work harder and are more successful. Gratitude is an essential leadership skill that must be genuine, intentional, and frequent.

Here's the continued benefit. Making gratitude part of our culture is contagious. Showing appreciation toward someone is likely to inspire that person to appreciate others. As we shift to the next ring of the flywheel, building strength, it's important to create inspiring workplaces where people openly appreciate each other. *Hardwiring Excellence in Education* presents several tools and tactics for leaders and teams to put into practice to create places where people are committed to and engaged in their work.

***Building Strength***

Organizations are excellent when employees do excellent work. The next ring of the flywheel is building strength in our people to strengthen our organization. That doesn't occur naturally; we need to be intentional with coaching and developing our people.

What's the key to building strength in our people? We make sure we

- communicate and demonstrate what is expected of employees.
- genuinely care about their well-being.
- listen and hear them.
- recognize their successes.
- provide feedback so they can improve.
- give them opportunities to develop their skills.
- challenge them to achieve beyond their own expectations.

Let's build strength in our people to hardwire the tools and tactics in this book that move our educational organizations from good to great. As Jim Collins says – "Good is the enemy of great." If you're reading this book, I have confidence you are someone who never settles for something to be good enough. You are always looking for ways to improve.

All nine principles require us to build leadership capacity in our organizations to achieve excellence. This part of the flywheel connects inspiring workplaces to results. We need the best from our people to be a high performing organization.

### *Accelerating Results*

Positive results turn the flywheel faster. We celebrate the wins while feeling energized to close performance gaps to stay on the winning side. We constantly improve, always focusing on getting better which builds momentum to take on new challenges.

Continuous checks on results lead to improvements being made. Continuous improvement conversations focus on applying strategies that move the organization forward. We know when we are achieving and when we are not. We use evidence to help us make good decisions and continue to test our applications. We celebrate improved results. When results slow or decline, we engage our teams in conversations about why the downturn is occurring and ways to improve.

All the while, people become more and more engaged in achieving the organizational goals. They see how what they do matters. How do we keep employees motivated? Engage them in conversations about what's working and why. Then shift the conversation to what's not working and why? Always ask them to answer with good evidence. Making improvement conversations part of our organizations motivates people.

Dr. Jennifer Lowery is the Superintendent of Tea Area School District, South Dakota. She is willing to take on new challenges to push herself, leaders, teachers, and staff. She leads with humility and a relentless focus on students and employees performing at their highest levels. I asked Dr. Lowery why it is important for her to lead this way. She said throughout her life people have opened doors for her. She is passionate about opening doors for others to learn and develop. She also expects her teams to be focused on the organizational goals. I asked her to give me an example of how this expectation plays out in her district. She said, *"Tea Area School District has been low performing in mathematics. Student performance in math is about 20% lower than reading. We are in a program improvement plan diving deep into this problem. We've found through our improvement cycles that students in some teachers' classrooms are outperforming the norm. Here's what these teachers are doing. They work with students to set goals together and apply quick checks on student performance. Students are asked to communicate how well they've performed by tracking their own achievement data."* Dr. Lowery talks about this process being part of the classroom Plan Do Study Act (PDSA) cycle that she learned from Dr. Pat Greco in the School District in Menomonee Falls and is now a proven solution we offer to our partner organizations. Dr. Lowery says, *"You will hear our students talk about how to get better by using data to analyze what they are doing well and where they need to improve."* When something is proven to work, Dr. Lowery is not afraid to standardize the work and train her team to apply the evidence-based practices. She has created an inspiring workplace focused on developing her people to achieve and accelerate results. That's what Dr. Lowery is passionate about. She works with that passion to lead her team.

*Hardwiring Excellence in Education* includes tools and tactics we can use to create inspiring workplaces, build strength in our people, and focus on achieving results by recognizing wins and determining areas to improve. The outer rings of the flywheel spin to connect us back to our educational core values – purpose, worthwhile work, and making a difference.

## A Key Factor that Stops the Flywheel

It takes focused work to get the flywheel spinning and keep it going. Even with all that work, there's one thing that can stop the flywheel from spinning – allowing a we/they culture to exist. When we communicate using we/they messages, we jeopardize the health of our organizations. We/they is a culture buster. It occurs when a leader or employee positions themselves positively at the expense of someone else. Leaders don't do this on purpose. In fact, we've all used we/they in our lives. We may not have known what we were doing or the negative impact of our behavior.

Looking back, when I was the dean of a college, I used we/they messages when I didn't want to share difficult information. At our university the administrators' offices were in Building 10. When I met with the chairs of our college departments or with faculty, I would say things like, *"If it were up to me, you would be able to hire a new team member but Building 10 didn't approve the new line."* Why did I do that? I wanted people to think positively about me, think that I fought for our college. By doing so, I positioned my supervisor and executives in a negative light. Now, I didn't intend to do that; nonetheless that was the undesirable outcome. Communicating using we/they messages doesn't help anyone in the long run. It destroys organizational culture.

Here's the difficult yet powerful message. We simply must stop communicating using we/they. Think of the different tone and outcome of my message if I had communicated to our college in this way – *"Our administration made some difficult decisions during a tight budget year. In looking at the data and decisions, I understand why the organizational leaders made certain decisions. Though we are not getting this new position, I am confident we will make it work with what we have. When comparing where we are and where we need to be, our job is to show higher growth to present the best case in the future. I'm committed to working with each of you to do just that."* Part of my job as the leader is to connect the dots for employees, and to do it in a way that creates unity, not division.

To shift away from we/they culture, we lead a culture of continuous improvement. Our teams buy into constantly trying to improve. They are dedicated to the relentless pursuit of getting better as an individual and team.

Nick Saban is one of the best coaches and leaders of all time. I bet we/they statements seldom occur. If something slips on the team, the negative behavior is called out and immediately stops. Saban leads with a culture of continuous improvement. He applies a coaching philosophy centered on a mental model called "process thinking." The emphasis for the team is placed on preparing for the game versus winning the game. The team executes each step of a process with diligence and precision, the desired outcome becomes expected. Coach Saban uses an acronym, WIN, which stands for "What's important now?" According to Saban, victory is improving moment by moment. At game time, it's all about executing each play with fidelity and precision in every moment. Saban learned to win by focusing on one play at a time to play the best football the team could play.

We all have our favorite college football teams. I graduated from Florida State University and am a tried-and-true FSU fan. As Florida State continues to improve under the leadership of a young coach, he too is focused on what it takes to improve one play at a time. That's a good lesson for us all to learn.

Great leaders always want to get better, one play at a time. They don't permit we/they messages that stop the spin of the organizational flywheel.

## You Can Always Get Better

I remember the first phone call with Dr. Pat Greco, a retired superintendent who is now a leader on our team. She is a leader of K12 improvement work modeling what improvement looks like from the boardroom to the classroom. As I was starting Studer Education, I had an opportunity to partner with Pat on building an excellent school district. She was leading her team to focus on classroom improvement but couldn't find a way to connect the dots to build an improvement approach in the districtwide offices. It's where we partnered to apply the Nine Principles Framework described in this book while she was the superintendent in the School District of Menomonee Falls, Wisconsin. Pat led that district to move from underperforming to becoming one of the highest performing districts in the country. The district is a Spotlight District for the Carnegie Foundation for the Advancement of Teaching. In this book, I highlight several examples where Pat and her leadership team applied the Nine Principles Framework to achieve excellence.

There are several phrases I hear Pat say that are cornerstones of improvement. First, we always focus on "getting better at getting better." Second, we focus on the "measures that matter" to guide leaders about where to make meaningful improvements. She focuses on engaging teams in improvement conversations as opposed to motivating teams using external threats of accountability. I've heard Pat say many times that in our K12 organizations we need to stop chasing shiny objects to find the magical solution and start applying an evidence-based approach to create an army of improvers to achieve positive results. With the great leadership of Superintendent Morgan, Hardin County Schools, KY is a great model for continuously focusing on improvement and using the "measures that matter" to drive meaningful conversations. On an *Accelerate Your Performance* Podcast episode, I asked Superintendent Morgan what has changed over the years as they have advanced their work. She said that prior to applying the tools and tactics described in this book, they led with a "spray and pray" approach, hoping that something they tried would be the solution that provided the results they were striving for. Today, they have a relentless and consistent focus on improvement.

A third phrase I hear Pat say is "Recognize the Bright Spots." I've seen her spotlight performance when she was the superintendent and now in her work with superintendents and leaders throughout the country. She's leveraging their work in publications and presentations at educational association meetings and conferences. She's a mentor to new superintendents and a trusted advisor to experienced ones. Her actions incentivize other superintendents and leaders to be at their best. And she does this by teaching leaders how to apply tools and tactics described in this book.

Pat teaches us to always be out in the field learning. And to always strive for ways to get better at using tools and tactics that turn the flywheel faster and faster.

Let's get your Organizational Flywheel spinning by applying the tools and tactics associated with the Nine Principles Framework described in each chapter. When educational leaders use the Nine Principles Framework, the Organizational Flywheel begins to turn with ever-increasing speed. As employees increasingly feel a sense of purpose and understand how their actions make a difference, anything begins to seem possible. The sky's the limit! Students feel cared for, safe and confident to achieve. Employees take pride in working for such an excellent organization, and they line up to work there. And families know their child is receiving an education that positions them to be successful.

# 1

# PRINCIPLE 1: COMMIT TO EXCELLENCE

*Set high expectations to achieve results while living out mission and values.*

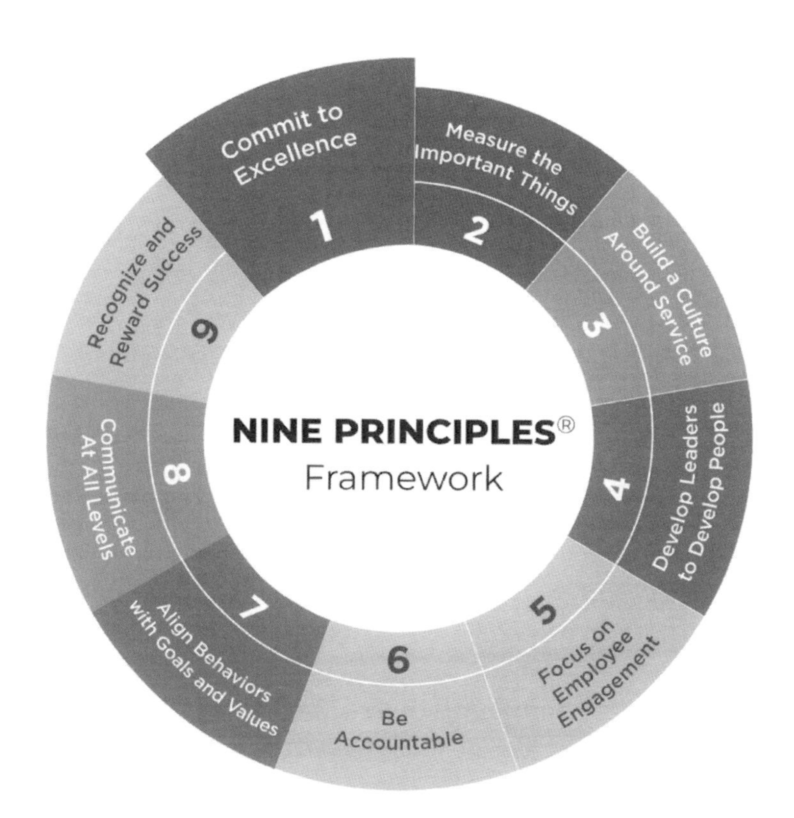

The first of the nine principles is Commit to Excellence. We commit to being the best at what we do. At times being average or good seems acceptable. After all, achieving at these levels requires diligent and focused work. Committing to being the best educational organization pushes leaders to focus relentlessly on improving daily.

Committing to excellence means we

- pay attention to every detail of our work.
- are aligned within our organization.
- consistently apply the most significant practices to help us achieve positive results.
- always know we can improve.
- provide the best services to students, families, and employees.

This chapter summarizes the foundational components for how we lead organizations by first committing to excellence. It includes operationalizing values, focusing on "people first," developing a strategic direction, and having an improvement mindset.

We start with defining and operationalizing our organizational values. As I've noted, the educational core values are having purpose, doing worthwhile work, and making a difference. That's what educators aspire to. To honor our educational core values, we connect them to our organizational core values by operationalizing what they look like when we are living them at work. Let's start with what it means to **operationalize the organizational values**. That's the first step to committing to excellence. We determine the organizational values that we want to live every day by describing what they look like in the workplace. In essence, our values shape the way we walk the halls rather than simply hanging on the walls.

## Operationalizing Values

What do we mean by operationalizing our values? As leaders, we

- clearly define what our values look like when people are doing a good job.
- apply a process for putting our values in action so the expected behaviors are clear.
- model for others what living the organizational values looks like.
- show that we are clear about what we believe and hold important.
- define teachable and observable behaviors used to develop people and hold them accountable for how to act and behave at work.

To accelerate these objectives, we design the Standards of Excellence to operationalize our values. As we develop the Standards of Excellence, we bring a group of high and solid performers together to lead the charge. We call this group the Standards of Excellence Team. We intentionally include employees who are on the front line interacting with students, families, and employees. The team engages in a process to create the draft Standards of Excellence. Although standards in various organizations are similar in nature, none of the Standards of Excellence is the same. That's because the standards represent the areas meaningful to a particular organization.

Our coaching team has facilitated hundreds of Standards of Excellence teams. Here's the process we use with organizations to create the Standards of Excellence. The Standards of Excellence (SoE) team engages in conversations with each other to develop a first draft of the standards. To achieve this goal, the SoE team

1. defines the value by asking, what does this value mean for our organization?
2. answers this question for each value, If we are living this value, what are the behaviors we are doing to demonstrate that value?
3. brainstorms, prioritizes, and refines key behaviors for each value.
4. continues to follow an iterative process that ends in draft Standards of Excellence for others to review.
5. shares the draft Standards of Excellence with the organizational leadership team for initial review and input.
6. surveys employees to gain their input on the draft Standards of Excellence gathering numeric and narrative feedback.
7. uses the employee feedback to refine and redraft the Standards of Excellence document.
8. sends the final draft to the leadership team.

The leadership team reviews and finalizes the Standards of Excellence and moves to official adoption by the organization. The last step is to launch the Standards of Excellence for all employees and new hires.

The Standards of Excellence are used to train and coach leaders and their teams; hold people accountable; and hire new team members who agree to live the values in the workplace. I provide four examples that demonstrate how leaders apply the Standards of Excellence in their organizations.

One of our partners, Northwestern Illinois Association (NIA), is a provider of special education services within their region. Jon Malone is the Executive Director of NIA. Northwestern Illinois Association was established in the late 1960s in response to new mandates for the provision of Special Education Services by public schools. Today NIA serves over 60 school districts in 10 Illinois counties. Jon and his team serve as a model for developing and applying the Standards of Excellence. Figure 3 shows the NIA Standards of Excellence. NIA Employees see these standards as the backbone of their organization. They are highly committed to being the best service provider to school districts.

## NORTHWESTERN ILLINOIS ASSOCIATION STANDARDS OF EXCELLENCE

### COLLABORATION

***Definition:*** We cultivate mutual respect and trust honest interactions that honor the uniqueness and dignity of all.

***Behaviors:*** All NIA team members will consistently demonstrate

- Active listening and active sharing to support team decisions
- Gratitude, encouragement, help and support for one another
- Team-based problem solving reflecting a professional and open attitude while considering multiple points of view
- 5/10 Rule (acknowledge others when passing within 10 feet, speak to others when passing within 5 feet)

**ACCOUNTABILITY**

***Definition:*** We accept ownership of performance and commitments through transparent communication and fiscally responsible decision-making.

***Behaviors:*** All NIA team members will consistently demonstrate:

- Follow through with commitments (Do what you say you will do)
- Commitment to results and process improvement
- "Touch back" within 24 hours of communication (respond to phone calls/emails within 24 hours to acknowledge receipt and provided anticipated timeline for response or solution)
- Carrying our own message directly to those involved
- Managing up (never throwing others under the bus)

**INNOVATION**

***Definition:*** We maximize student success through creativity, specialized services, and expertise.

***Behaviors:*** All NIA team members will demonstrate:

- Consistent openness to change and growth resulting in better student outcomes or better service to customers (openness to change is sharing ideas, considering all viewpoints, giving an honest effort to support a decision or new process, sharing results)
- Sharing of innovative or research-based best practices formally and informally with internal and external customers.
- Articulation and application of new learning to foster organizational and student growth.

**INTEGRITY**

***Definition:*** We act in a truthful, ethical, and professional manner to build strong partnerships.

***Behaviors:*** All NIA team members will consistently demonstrate:

- Sharing of decision-making with our team and our customers – with them and not to them (shared is defined as collecting information and input, sharing the why, and focusing on clarity)
- Proactive transparent communication with stakeholders around purpose, processes, and results
- Ownership of performance, results, and mistakes (treating questions and concerns respectfully)

*Figure 3. Northwestern Illinois Association Standards of Excellence*

Jon has received one of Studer Education's outstanding leadership awards – the Difference Maker Award. I presented the award to Jon, which he humbly accepted at our annual "What's Right in Education" conference. He sent me a note asking if I would get on a zoom call with his NIA team to present the award so that he could accept it on behalf of the NIA employees who are living the Standards of Excellence. His coach, Dr. KK Owen, and I had the pleasure of presenting the Difference Maker Award to his team. Now, that's a great example of a leader and organization being their best.

One of our community college partners, South Louisiana Community College (SLCC), followed the development process presented in this chapter early on in their excellence journey. The college had undergone a merger between two different colleges in the Acadiana region. We first worked together to create a new strategic plan, including developing collective values. The standards development process pulled together a diverse group of employees to develop the SLCC Standards of Excellence. With the complicated change of merging two organizations, SLCC developed a comprehensive set of standards. They used the standards to create a positive culture. I first worked with Dr. Natalie Harder, the former Chancellor, and the Human Resources Executive, Alicia Hulin, to launch the Standards of Excellence. Dr. Harder has now assumed the Presidency at Coker University, South Carolina where we have an opportunity to partner with this university.

Dr. Vincent June was hired as the new SLCC Chancellor. He brings his experience and expertise to take the college to the next level. The Standards of Excellence (Figure 4) remain solid in defining the SLCC culture. In times of leadership change, the Standards of Excellence remain constant in the culture as the institutional leaders manage change. Under Dr. June's leadership, Alicia Hulin has expanded her role as the leader of strategic initiatives and engagement. In this role, she uses the standards to design the learning outcomes for professional development sessions with staff and managers. SLCC also uses the standards to hire new employees and evaluate employee performance. Dr. June has advanced the standards with his leadership team to design eight SLCC leadership priorities defining leadership expectations at SLCC. These leadership priorities are applied in the executive team strategy retreats and Leadership Development Institutes in support of leaders modeling behaviors identified in the SLCC Standards of Excellence.

## SOUTH LOUISIANA COMMUNITY COLLEGE STANDARDS OF EXCELLENCE

The goal of South Louisiana Community College is to be excellent. Excellence occurs when we are passionate and deliberate about developing quality programs; recruiting and retaining high-performing leaders, faculty, and staff; and graduating students who will successfully take their next step into the workforce or continuing their education. We also commit to being excellent by living our values through our standards.

### ACCOUNTABILTY

***Definition:*** Occurs when we create a work environment that supports employees reaching their highest potential and sets the stage for building a culture of excellence and continuous improvement.

***Behaviors:***

- Commit to doing what is promised
- Own mistakes without shifting blame to others.
- Own problems that surface without shifting to others.
- Pay attention to details and all aspects of a task that must be done.
- Take responsibility for doing a good job by being accurate and thorough with any job at hand.
- Do work with a “can do” attitude.

---

**COLLABORATION**

***Definition:*** Occurs when we champion and partner with our students, colleagues, and communities that include communicating and partnering with programs, departments, business and industry, educational institutions, and communities.

***Behaviors:***

- Seek input from others and value others' opinions and ideas.
- Work together and not against each other.
- Proactively work together within units and across units to achieve common goals.
- Be open to feedback and input from others.
- Consider and value different perspectives.
- Display a positive and empathetic attitude toward others.
- Work together in a support manner by being dependable, trustworthy, and flexible.

---

**INNOVATION**

***Definition:*** Occurs when we aim to be relevant and build creative and efficient solutions in the core institutional areas (instructional, student affairs/services, adult education, operations/finance), knowing that "place" and "community" are important to students and residents and are what drive us.

***Behaviors:***

- Value the culture in the region to inspire creativity.
- Collectively engage people with diverse ideas to think about to do things in new and improved ways.
- Approach change as an opportunity and with appreciation.
- Identify opportunities in our region and provide solutions.
- Deploy leading edge technology, employee development programs, and process improvement tools.

---

**INTEGRITY**

***Definition:*** Occurs when we commit to being honest by saying what we mean, matching our behaviors to our words, and taking responsibility for our actions.

***Behaviors:***

- Work each day by applying high standards.
- Do the right things, even when no one is looking.
- Be open about why decisions are made and why actions are taken.
- Communicate in a way that does not mislead people.
- Engage with others by being courteous and conscientious and with professional appearance.

---

**RESPECT**

***Definition:*** Occurs when we nurture a safe workplace environment of mutual respect and shared decision-making with opportunities for all employees to be engaged.

***Behaviors:***

- Be sincere.
- Maintain confidentiality, and respect privacy at all times.
- Listen actively without interruption and without judgment.
- Ask questions to seek a clear understanding of a particular situation.
- Use the most appropriate form of communication for the situation.
- Engage in honest two-way communication.

---

**SERVICE**

***Definition:*** Occurs when those we serve achieve their goals by taking the "next step" of their future. Doing so means we focus on what is best for those we serve, including a focus on processes, decisions, operational structures, quality instruction, and student success.

***Behaviors:***

- Use a pleasant tone and approach with others (students, peers, community, etc.).
- Focus decisions and work on satisfying "customer."
- Be student-centered by remembering that everything we do focuses on creating a valuable student experience.
- Put people first - treat everyone with care and respect.
- Build trusting relationships with students, our communities, and each other.
- Work with students to help them succeed to gain employment and/or continue with their education.

---

**TRUST**

***Definition:*** Occurs when our employees, students, and communities work toward common goals, show respect toward each other, and fulfill our commitments; it is a choice we make toward someone when we are inspired that they have earned our confidence.

***Behaviors:***

Be honest, even when it is difficult to do.

Communicate the right message in the right way at the right time for the right reasons.

Keep people in the information loop – changes, good things, improvements.

Be clear about intentions by being open and honest and staying true to commitments.

Invest in employees to grow and achieve and apply fair practices when they do not.

Explain why things are being done.

*Figure 4. South Louisiana Community College Standards of Excellence*

The third example involves students being involved in operationalizing the core values. Dr. Mark Bielang, also a Difference Maker Award recipient, is the Superintendent of Portage Public Schools, Michigan. The school district enrolls about 9,000 students. Dr. Bielang wanted a team to design the standards by defining the core values and developing actions/behaviors that demonstrate each value. He selected an initial Values Team to begin the work. Dr. Bielang expanded the initiative to include the voice of students. He leveraged a long-standing "Superintendent's Student Advisory Board" to begin the conversation about what mattered in Portage Public Schools. Here's what's important about his leadership. The students and his employees see him as a listening and learning leader. The students trusted him enough to engage in honest and thoughtful conversations. Like the way he engages with his leaders and employees, Dr. Bielang empowers students to speak up and participate fully.

The last example shows how another organization embeds the Standards of Excellence to define the organizational culture. Dr. Sally Sugg is the superintendent of Shelby County Public Schools, Kentucky. She led a process that spread throughout the district and educational community. Shelby County Public Schools (SCPS) serves about 7,000 students. Prior to Dr. Sugg serving as the superintendent of schools, the district did not have core values. She led the development of the district core values that became an integral part of their most recent Strategic Leadership Plan. The core values of Accountability, Empathy, Growth Mindset, Integrity, Professionalism, and Teamwork were collaboratively identified and defined by all employees in the district. The Standards of Excellence defining the core values for SCPS is called Shelby Inspired: Learning, Leading, and Living.

In the district, leaders go first, and leaders model the expectations. Therefore, monthly leadership development (Lead & Learn) sessions incorporate the core values. Modeling the standards starts at the top. Dr. Sugg visited each school to introduce the operationalized core values. The district asked school-based leaders to manage-up individuals who demonstrated the SCPS Core Values in their everyday actions. This afforded the Board of Education, district, and school leadership the opportunity to recognize individuals publicly for their commitment to their values. The end of year celebration culminated with six individuals being recognized as district representatives for each of the core values.

Initially, it was thought that having all employees become aware of and implement the SCPS Core Values would take some time due to the volume of employees. The exact opposite occurred. The SCPS Core Values are driving the work and serving as a common thread throughout the district. What began as employee values has expanded to students, parents, and the community.

As you can see from the examples, committing to excellence is about being a great organizational citizen. Leaders and employees commit to

- the educational core values – purpose, worthwhile work, and making a difference in the lives of others.
- operationalizing the organizational values to design Standards of Excellence.

Living with a Commitment to Excellence requires leaders to model the behaviors outlined in the standards and to be dedicated to helping others be their best. That's how we put people first. We operationalize and live the organizational core values to build inspiring workplaces that strengthen the skills of our employees.

## People First

In the book, *BE 2.0 (Beyond Entrepreneurship 2.0),* Jim Collins recalls a conversation with Steve Jobs about Apple coming out of the dark days to emerge as an industry leader. Jim Collins asked, what did you build upon to emerge from darkness? What gave you hope? Collins thought Jobs was going to answer with some great innovative idea. But that's not what Jobs talked about at all. He talked about finding the right people in the company to help build the turnaround. He found people who still had the burning passion for the "change-the-world" vision. Jobs learned that the only way to build an enduring company that makes the best products is to have the right people working in the right culture.

Collins continues by proposing that the number one priority for any organization to be excellent is to get the key seats on the bus filled with the right people. He tells us if less than 90% of key seats are not filled by the right people, we have identified our top priority. The goal is not 100% because at any given time people will naturally be making professional decisions, or changes occurring in the organization will shift people around or out.

Leaders fill key seats on the bus. To be excellent, leaders must have the skills and live the organizational values. The Nine Principles Framework provides a recipe for effective leadership skills. The tools and tactics described in each chapter focus on leaders balancing the emotional and rational sides of our organizations. Years ago, psychologist Jonathan Haidt introduced a useful analogy for thinking about behavior change. Haidt argues that we have two sides: an emotional side (the Elephant), and a rational side (its Rider). In their book, *Switch*, Chip and Dan Heath expanded on this concept. They ask us to picture a rider holding the reigns perched on top of an elephant traveling down a defined path. (Figure 5). The rider guides the elephant down the path. In a moment the elephant and the rider disagree about the direction to go, the rider is going to lose the battle and will steer off course.

As leaders, we tend to spend most of our time on the rational part of our jobs without tending to the emotional part of our workplace. Yet, the workplace emotion is much stronger and bigger than any rational aspect of the work. To travel down the right path and have the agility to make meaningful changes, we must understand our people and help them travel the path with us. Leaders define the paths to travel, develop people to move forward, and tune into how they are doing along the way. Leaders travel the organizational path by putting people first. To do so, they know what their employees expect from them.

*Figure 5. Elephant and the Rider*

What do people want from their leaders? They want leaders who act in a calm and determined way to lead teams to greatness. They also want to follow someone who has an unwavering resolve to do what needs to be done to lead teams to success, especially through the most difficult times. Teams will follow leaders they respect. These leaders

- model what they expect of others.
- develop and promote people.
- give credit to others.
- get in the trenches to do the hard work.
- make others feel important.
- thank people at every opportunity.

Leaders who put people first gain trust. People like to follow their lead. Trust is earned by their actions. Attending to the elephant builds trust along the excellence journey taking one step at time.

I talked about how Mark Bielang, the superintendent of Portage Public Schools, empowered employees and students to design the district's Standards of Excellence. This example plus others I will outline serve as examples of a leader who puts people first. Simply put, Mark empowers people in his organization. Working with his coach Dr. KK Owen, he gives equal professional development time to various professional sectors in the school district. The mantra at Portage Public Schools is "everyone is a leader here."

Mark and KK work with the Executive Leadership Team on high level initiatives such as district, department and school scorecards described in Chapter 7. Mark positions his executive team to function like a "think tank." He is a participant and a listener. He encourages and participates in frank discussions. He values everyone around the table by listening intently. He guides the team to make clear decisions and uses data to guide improvement discussions.

Mark spends time with the administrative teams in schools and departments tackling prickly themes such as employee, student, family, and service excellence survey results using the survey roll put process outlined in Chapters 3 and 5. In addition, Mark works alongside KK to teach specific and timely leadership skills, such as "just in time listening skills" and "how to take care of yourself as a leader while leading during tough times." Mark doesn't direct these groups; he is an active participant with the administrative team. He is a listener, learner, and participant. He serves in this same role at leader and staff training sessions focused on service excellence and workplace culture. Mark's behavior shows he puts people first. Consequently, his employees trust him and are engaged in learning, growing, and developing their leadership skills, many of which are summarized in this book.

Putting people first means developing everyone to be a leader. The tools and tactics in this book show how putting people first is a prerequisite to being an excellent organization. We may equate putting people first to "soft skills" that tend to get brushed to the side. They may be soft skills, but they are so darn hard to do consistently. Also, the concepts of the nine principles aren't necessarily anything new. They provide better ways to apply necessary practices to get improved organizational results. What makes this book different is that I focus on specific actions anyone can take in organizations to develop the leadership skills that have a direct impact on improving the workplace culture and achieving high performing results.

## Strategic Direction

To align our behaviors to this principle, we operationalize our values, put people first, and focus on a strategic direction. Key leaders set the strategic direction of an organization to tee up a strategic planning process. To evolve and grow, remain strong and relevant, the key leaders must understand the current state and industry trends that factor into what an organization needs to become.

Key leaders answer these questions.

- In the next 5 to 10 years, what do we want to become to align to current major and predicted industry trends?
- Where are we now? Where do we need to go?
- How do we need to continuously evolve and change?
- Why is it important to our organization to travel this path to the future?

The strategic direction serves as the north star for designing the organizational "pillars" of excellence, which represent descriptive and measurable themes that define organizational priorities. Organizations first start with something like a commitment statement, Big Aims, or a succinctly defined vision. The pillars represent the thematic priorities for living out the underlying organizational commitment. Therefore, the pillars are the foundation for building a roadmap to a successful future in the design of the strategic plan.

Here's an example from the University of West Georgia. Dr. Brendan Kelly worked with his executive team to set the strategic direction of the institution that guided the strategic planning process. The executive team drafted the commitment statement and the strategic priorities or pillars to leverage conversations with various audiences about the future of UWG. The commitment statement is - The University of West Georgia commits to "dedicating ourselves to the curation of a first-choice university." The strategic plan also includes three pillars.

**Relevance:** UWG will continue to evolve to be more relevant to students' needs (both inside and outside the classroom), as well as adapting to a changing world and economy.

**Competitiveness:** UWG curates its operations around higher end-user expectations to emerge as the first choice for students, employees, employers, alumni and supporters.

**Place-making:** A public university is a unique institution in the United States that has the capacity to provide a holistic "sense of place." UWG will live up to that expectation all the time.

In our work with partner organizations, many apply common pillars, including student success, workplace environment, service excellence, health and safety, and finance. As part of the strategic planning process, each organization designs an overall purpose or commitment statement and aligns the definitions of the pillars to the overall organizational direction indicated by this purpose.

We use the commitment of the organization and pillars to facilitate a strategic planning process. Our goal is to engage in meaningful conversations with leaders, faculty, staff, and community partners to gain insight on what needs to be considered to live the strategic vision and direction.

To guide the data collection and analysis processes, we select a Strategic Planning Team that represents a cross section of the organization. We invite a core team of about 10 to 15 people to serve as members of the team. We choose people who have a deep understanding of the organization, are invested in its well-being, and excited about being part of the future.

We hold discovery or input sessions with various groups of people to collect insights from those we serve. The team starts with summarizing the strategic direction of the organization referring to the commitment statement and pillars. Then they ask three questions.

- If we are living out this direction, what will success look like in the next 3 to 5 years?
- How will we know we've been successful?
- What do we need to focus on in the next 3 to 5 years to be successful? and why?

Our coaches guide the Strategic Planning Team to analyze the information gathered, develop themes, and summarize supporting thoughts to the themes. After completing the data collection and analysis process with the team, a draft document is developed to include the strategic direction, pillars, and goal statements for each pillar. The team provides the draft document to the senior leaders to share with key leaders. Together they continue to draft and finalize the strategic plan. The final strategic plan is a one- to two- page guide that leaders share with internal and external audiences affiliated with the organization. Leaders use the strategic plan to make key decisions to move the organization forward in a positive direction.

Every year, leaders use the strategic plan to operationalize annual goals and strategic actions to achieve the goals. I've watched our coaches work with leaders to bring strategic plans to life. I had the pleasure of working with the University of West Georgia (UWG) to facilitate their strategic planning process. The executive team set the strategic direction and theme for the planning process. The core driver of the UWG Strategic Plan is "BECOMING is about what we grow to be." The UWG commitment statement and pillars presented above drove the conversations with input groups.

UWG followed the process outlined in this chapter to create a highly focused strategic plan that guides people at the institution to create outcomes influencing the work that matters. The Strategic Planning Team sought the input and support of members across the UWG community to shape this comprehensive blueprint for the university, one that provides clarity and relevance for the future of the institution. More than 1,300 members of the UWG community - students, faculty, staff, alumni, community leaders, boards, and other external stakeholders - took an active role in the university's strategic planning for the future.

Today, UWG leaders continuously connect their actions to this plan. They focus on ways to improve. Conversations naturally occur in alignment with the strategic vision, commitment statement, and strategic priorities/pillars with aligned goals. UWG leaders are focused on solid execution of the strategic plan described in Chapters 2 and 7. They've applied an improvement approach that focuses people's attention on how they can get better and better to be a "first choice" university for students.

## Improvement Mindset

The final focus area for committing to excellence is working with an improvement mindset. An improvement mindset means we are always looking for ways to get better. We celebrate actions that are working, and we do more of them. We turn challenges into opportunities and identify ways to solve problems that impede progress. We focus more on improvement and less on accountability. Why? Because if we continuously improve, we are more likely to achieve our desired results. Accountability then is the outcome of our improvements rather than a threatening way to lead people.

Improvement motivates people. Most people want to have goals and ways to improve to achieve those goals. Engaging our people in improvement conversations leads to a more highly engaged workforce. We get better when we know the goal, talk about what's working, what's not working, and how we can work together to improve.

We commit to excellence when we come to work every day with an improvement mindset. We always believe there's room for improvement. The other eight principles show how to put our improvement mindset into action. The first principle reinforces the need for leaders to instill an improvement mindset in their organizations.

The most successful leaders are those who lead with an improvement mindset. They thrive on a challenge and see failure as a springboard for growth. It's so easy for us to say; yet so difficult to do. I don't know about you, but I like what it feels like to achieve goals. However, some of the biggest growth opportunities have been when I didn't succeed.

I'm reminded of a time when I played in a tennis tournament in my mid-20s. I had just moved back to Pensacola, didn't know many people, and hadn't hung out with a tennis team or crowd before deciding to enter a tournament. I played tennis in high school and loved the sport. At the time of the tournament, I was entering my first year of teaching. I couldn't afford a tennis wardrobe or to belong to a tennis club. I still had my old K-Swiss white tennis shoes. They stayed with me so long in life, it was difficult to depart with them when they were falling apart. I entered the court realizing that my opponent played at the club. She had a cheering section watching her.

We started the match. The spectators (my opponent's friends) were surprised at how well I could play. I played beautifully until the final point of each game. When it came time for me to win a game, I choked.......every time at every game. I lost the match with a 6 – 0, 6 – 0 score. I was humiliated and deflated. I went to the net to shake hands with my opponent. When she shook my hand, she said, *"You are a talented player, but you are your own worst enemy. Your lack of confidence in your abilities keeps you from winning."* I will never forget that moment. It motivated me to improve.

I carried this comment with me into leadership. When the odds are stacked against my team and me, I tell myself –

NOT to be my own worst enemy. I've learned over the years that an improvement mindset overcomes failures.

## Chapter 1 Summary

In 2008, I sat in a conference called "Take You and Your Organization to the Next Level" or TYYO. I heard the initial version of the nine principles presented by Quint Studer. The nine principles were life changing for me. I'm grateful for being introduced to them. Leaving the TYYO conference I had tools and tactics to help me continue to grow. I attended every TYYO conference thereafter taking copious notes and learning more each time. Today, I've had the opportunity to update and apply the Nine Principles Framework to continuously improve my leadership abilities, always striving for excellence. Also, I am fortunate to share this framework with other leaders who commit to excellence.

Hearing the nine principles encouraged me to make a major career decision. After 20 years, I left the University of West Florida to start Studer Education. It gave me a chance to work with educational organizations to refine the Nine Principles Framework to align to education and service-focused industries. Gaining momentum over the years, we've worked with some of the best organizations in the country and hired some of the best people on our team to lead the Nine Principles Framework movement. Principle 1: Commit to Excellence lays the foundation for improving ourselves, each other, and our organization to be the best. We lay the groundwork for the excellence journey by operationalizing the organizational values, putting people first, setting the strategic direction of the organization, and working every day with an improvement mindset. Let's continue to learn the tools and tactics aligned to each principle to travel this excellence journey.

# 2

# MEASURES THAT MATTER

*Continuously track progress to achieve results with an improvement mindset.*

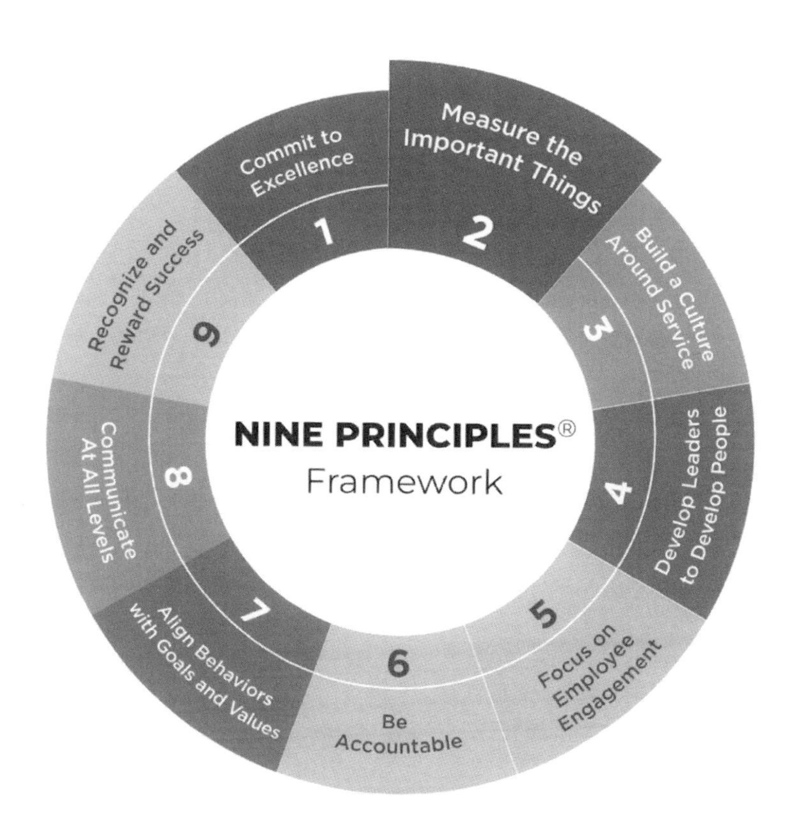

The strategic plan outlines the vision, direction, and objectives of the organization. Now we focus on executing the plan. The organizational pillars from the strategic plan provide the framework for establishing the measures that matter. The measures that matter drive the top priorities, define organizational success, and direct us on the most important work to do. That is, we know what priorities to work on and where to spend our time.

To sort out the organizational priorities, I've worked with leaders to complete an Organizational Growth Bull's Eye. I really love this tool. It provides a good first step to engage leaders in meaningful discussions to move from strategy to execution. As leaders, it helps us answer this question - what are our winning moves to achieve positive results in the short and long-term? The completed Bull's Eye also guides us on how we differentiate what we do. The pillars on our strategic plan may be somewhat the same across organizations, but the priorities we focus on depend on the uniqueness of our organizations. It also keeps us from thinking initiatives like "giving all students a digital tool" represent winning moves that directly produce results. Providing technology to students may be an ingredient for achieving success, but that act alone will not result in higher student performance. The Bull's Eye guides leaders to focus their attention on priorities that lend themselves to producing the best results (Figure 6).

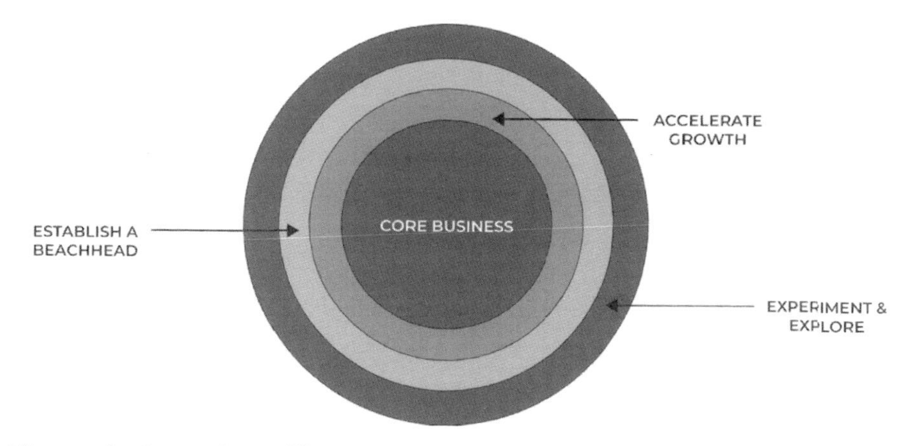


*Figure 6. Growth Bull's Eye*

The Bull's Eye contains 4 rings that have specific questions. Dr. Rick Bateman, Jr., the Chancellor of Bossier Parish Community College (BPCC) led his team to apply the Bull's Eye to determine the most important priorities for growing their institution and serving students well. The senior leadership team answered the questions associated with each ring of the Bull's Eye.

- The inner ring is labeled *Core Business*: What do we offer to students right now that keeps us in business and contributes to the bottom line?
- The second ring is labeled *Accelerate to Grow*. What are our winning moves to grow our bottom line? What do we focus on that will help us accelerate growth and will become part of our core business?
- The third ring is labeled *Establish a Beachhead*: Where is there an opening in the market to meet business & industry needs that we can address with the goal of moving to accelerate growth?
- The fourth ring is labeled *Experiment and Explore*: Where do we want to invest in potential strategic opportunities to see if there is a path to grow?

BPCC is a model for how they developed their institutional Bull's Eye. They use it to align their "measures that matter" and annualized strategic actions across divisions. They focus 90% of their attention on the first two rings (proven areas they want to continue to execute and areas where they are getting improved results to fold into their core work). The leadership team is focused on about 10% of actions associated with the beachhead ring. A beachhead is where leaders focus limited resources on areas that have potential for advancing a stronghold on results. BPCC is investing most of the resources in areas where they want to double down on their core programs and accelerate growth where they have completed the legwork for understanding the demands and trends in the workforce.

Over the years, BPCC has laid a solid foundation for building a positive culture, hiring talented leaders, developing their senior leadership team, staying focused on industry market trends in their community and state, and focusing on providing students with various types of personal and academic support through their Cavalier Care Center. This foundation sets the stage for BPCC leaders to execute to the Strategic Bull's Eye to advance the institution.

Later in the chapter, I share how Dr. Casey Blochowiak improved processes to break down barriers that impeded elementary students from achieving improved math results. Casey is currently a leader coach on our Studer Education team. She retired from the School District of Menomonee Falls where she led the teaching and learning division. To better prepare for completing a scorecard process to continuously track progress toward results, Casey wanted to make sure she and her team were focused on the right priorities and actions. That's what the Organizational Growth Bull's Eye guides leaders to do. Here's how Casey and her team completed the divisional Bull's Eye.

At the center of the Bull's Eye, the district defined what they were striving to be the best at doing. They were striving to be best-in-class in college and career readiness. Everything they placed as an academic priority was connected to how it drove college and career readiness. Casey led her teaching and learning division to aggressively develop and grow tried-and-true practices. These actions are in the second ring of the Bull's Eye. The district had tested the strategies, reviewed the results, and modified the strategies to become some of their "winning moves." Most of these actions focused on K-5 literacy and math and core academic opportunities for the high school core curriculum. The actions included

- K12 Strategic Coaching.
- K-1 Phonics.
- K-5 Literacy/Math Curriculum.
- K-5 Literacy/Math Tier 3 Interventions.
- High School AP Access and Achievement.
- High School Academies.
- High Literacy Always Actions (consistent must dos).

The district also launched Beachhead areas to continue to apply, test, and assess before fully executing the strategy. The priorities included

- K-5 Learning Journals.
- K-5 Social Studies.
- 2nd Grade Phonics Pilot.
- Middle School Electives Alignment.
- Middle School Journals.
- Middle School Literacy/Writing.
- Middle School & High School Math Best Practices.
- High School Rise.
- High School Career Based Learning.

Casey led her team to hardwire excellence on strategies in the accelerate to grow and beachhead rings of the Bull's Eye. They had a list of possible areas in the experiment and explore ring of the Bull's Eye. However, the district first focused on consistently executing the priorities in the accelerate to grow areas and continued modifying the beachhead priorities until ready to shift up to the next level of the Bull's Eye.

The strategic plan and bull's eye serve as foundational reference tools for leaders to check how well they are focused on the defined priorities of the organization. The Bull's Eye keeps us honest in making good decisions about the academic strategies we elect to execute across the board. From this point, we apply a scorecard process to define the "measures that matter," determine the actions to work on to achieve the goals and create the progress measures to track our progress. The measures on the scorecard should show a direct connection to the priorities in the first two rings of the Bull's Eye.

Scorecard measures include both lag and lead measures. We first identify the annual measurable goals for each pillar. Annual measures indicate the goal we are trying to achieve. These are mostly lag measures, which tell us if we've achieved a goal. For each of the pillars and measurable goals, we also include progress measures or lead measures, which tell us how likely we are to achieve the goal. Lead measures serve as predictors of success.

This chapter provides tools and tactics for Principle 2 Measures that Matter. I will describe an organizational scorecard process and how to use that process to improve. Our initial goal is to identify meaningful organizational measures that drive the right behaviors to achieve results. This chapter also includes how the scorecard informs when failed processes impede progress toward achieving goals.

## Organizational Scorecard Measures

We've found that most key success areas in education focus on student success, people, service, safety, and finance. To operationalize the strategic plan, leaders first determine the measures that matter that define success. As we create measures for each pillar, let's keep this rule of thumb in mind that Stephen Covey recommends.

- Selecting two to three measures per pillar gives us a good chance of achieving the goals.
- Selecting four to ten measures reduces our chance of achieving one to two goals.
- Selecting eleven or more goals reduces our chance of hitting any goal.

Let's apply this rule of thumb by developing no more than two to three measures for each pillar on the scorecard. The pillars represent distinct areas of focus that indirectly connect to each other. For example, by taking care of employees, we have a better chance of improving student achievement and parent satisfaction. The annual measures set the targets. The progress measures inform us about how well we are doing on the targets throughout the year. Solely focusing on lag measures leaves hitting goals to chance. Progress measures give us an opportunity to determine where we need to improve before it's too late. They inform us of the actions we need to take to improve. Therefore, once leaders establish the overall measures, they answer two questions, What are the key actions to help us achieve the goal? and What are key lead measures to indicate our progress toward achieving the goals?

Let's review how the scorecard process (annual measures, progress measures, key actions) applies to a measure from the People Pillar. Let's say a district wants to increase the mean score on a certain question on the employee engagement survey from 3.50 to 3.75 on a 5-point scale. The district wants to improve the score on the item, "I recommend that families send their children to a school in our district." Over time, they want this score to be one of the highest. They want people who work in the district to feel they work at a place they would recommend to families. Therefore, they focus on two key strategy actions.

- All leaders engage in a discussion with teachers and staff during their employee engagement roll out meetings (more on this in Chapter 5). After that discussion and review of input, each leader communicates the 1 to 3 actions that have the best opportunity to improve results.
- All leaders do purposeful leader rounding with their teams (more on this in Chapter 5). As part of the rounding session, leaders ask, what are we doing that helps you recommend our district to families? What is occurring that reduces your confidence to recommend the district to families?

To check their progress on these actions, each leader administers a one question assessment to their teams every 60 days, asking, on a scale of 1 to 5, to what extent would you recommend our school district as a place for families to send their children. The results are analyzed and shared with their teams to gain input. The leaders may use the results to refine the key actions as they go.

In this example, the district has an annual measure (the overall end of year mean score). They have aligned key actions and a way to gather progress measures (the score on one survey item every 60 days) to determine what's working and where they need to continue to improve on the People Pillar.

The scorecard is a key tool for executing a plan. It can be developed at the district, school, and department levels. The scorecard includes pillars, definitions of pillars, annual measures, progress measures and key actions. Figure 7 provides an example of some possible annual results measures and aligned progress measures and key actions for a district scorecard focused on three pillars – student achievement, service, and people.

The district scorecard is used to create scorecards for all schools and departments. The department directors and school leaders will look at the district expectations and align their unit's goals and actions to the district scorecard. All leaders will be working with their teams to achieve their goals, which in turn will help the district. Therefore, leaders and staff know what it takes to achieve success, how progress will be tracked, and what teams and individuals will do to achieve organizational excellence. This cascading process is described in more detail in Chapter 7.

We recommend that about every 45 to 75 days, leaders meet to review their progress toward achieving the defined "measures that matter" outlined on the scorecards. The leadership team reviews the progress data and engages in conversations to determine if the key actions are achieving above, at, or below goal. This conversation directs them on what to keep doing, stop doing, and do differently.

To initiate this discussion, we can apply a plus/delta approach. As we review progress measures, we ask what's working and where we have opportunities to improve? We may ask, *What are we confident about that is working? How do we know?* Our goal is to learn what to keep doing and do more of. This information guides leaders on where to provide training to get their teams' behaviors and actions aligned to

| STUDENT ACHIEVEMENT | PEOPLE | SERVICE |
|---|---|---|
| Every student will be college- and career- ready | Provide an inspiring work environment so people can be their best at work | Provide amazing service to internal and external "customers" |
| ***Annual Results Measures*** | | |
| Increase the proficiency level for district-wide mathematics achievement to score at the highest level on the state report card | Improve the "recommend" score on the employee engagement survey from 3.99 to 4.20 | Improve parent satisfaction survey from 4.28 to 4.33 |
| Increase the proficiency level for district-wide literacy achievement to score at the highest level on the state report card | Increase employee attendance by 20% | Improve internal support services survey from 4.21 to 4.31 |
| Improve student engagement survey from 4.10 to 4.25 | | |

| **Progress Measures** | | |
|---|---|---|
| 60-day benchmark assessment for every student | 60-day assessments of the one survey question for all schools and departments | 60-day one question survey to randomly surveyed families |
| 85% of students will score a C or above in their courses | Daily attendance | Reduce costs by 2% from providing more efficient services by departments within the district |
| 90% daily attendance | | |
| ***Key Actions*** | | |
| Implement Plan, Do, Study, Act (PDSA) for all grades; apply a common process for data retreats by leaders at schools | All leaders follow the plan to round with employees and track on a stoplight report | All teachers make one positive phone call home to parents every week following a plan to connect with all parents |
| Assign literacy and math coaches for supporting the lowest performing students | Administer and roll out the employee survey and focus on school and department actions that roll up to district actions | Apply service rounding using the feedback on the Support Services Excellence Survey Results |

*Figure 7. Sample Organizational Scorecard*

produce positive results. We also ask, *Who can we recognize that helped us move in a positive direction?* This gives us an opportunity to recognize people that others can learn from. We then ask, *Where are we experiencing challenges and why?* Continuously reviewing the data helps us know where we need to adjust our actions to improve. More detail on the 45- to 75-day improvement cycle is described in Chapter 7.

## Process Improvements

It's difficult to achieve positive results when we fail to have good processes in place to act on the measures that matter. The scorecard execution process can help improve broken processes. When difficult barriers arise, we want to study the deeper problems that are getting in the way of achieving positive results. Some problems are quickly solved; others require deeper exploration and experimentation.

We start by asking, *What is getting in the way of achieving positive results?* As we review the progress results, we specifically define the problem that needs to be solved and make sure the problem has a potential solution. We then ask, *Why is this problem occurring?* Our goal is to get to the root cause of the problem so that we can find a good solution.

One way to find the root cause of a problem is to apply a method called the 5 Whys. Dr. Casey Blochowiak, one of our leader coaches and a former Director of Curriculum and Instruction in the School District of Menomonee Falls, Wisconsin shared this example with our team. She, the 8th grade principal, and a team of teachers were reviewing one of the major pain points in the district for several years - 8th grade math proficiency rates on the state assessment (annual scorecard measure). She noticed that the team was quick to jump to solutions without slowing down and fully assessing the situation. As educators, we are in the problem-solving business so it's natural for teams to go straight to finding solutions.

Casey remembers slowing the conversation by applying the 5 Whys approach to lead the team to find the root cause of the problem. The team engaged in a year and half project addressing the "root of the problem."

Here's what the 5 Why's approach looked like. The first step is to state the challenge: Continued low proficiency rates in 8th grade mathematics on the state assessment. Then the team engaged in a conversation following this line of questioning.

- Why is this challenge occurring?
  *Why 1 answer - There are gaps between what we are teaching and what is being tested.*
- Why are these gaps occurring?
  *Why 2 answer - Our 8th grade math curriculum (Algebra 1) does not fully align to the Wisconsin state standards.*
- Why doesn't the Algebra 1 curriculum align to the state standards?
  *Why 3 answer – The Algebra 1 course was district designed by the High School math team.*
- Why is the design a problem?
  *Why 4 answer – At the time of the last curriculum adoption, Algebra 1 was primarily a high school course. Now, most students take Algebra 1 as an 8th grader.*
- Why is the change along with the other decisions causing a problem?
  *Why 5 answer - We decreased the barrier for accessing advanced courses but did not address the alignment to standards tightly.*

The team used the answers to the 5 why questions to define the root cause of the problem and began determining the best possible solution to test. Here's what they summarized. They needed to align the Algebra 1 curriculum to the standards that students are expected to master at each grade-level. Then determine as a district if they were going to adopt the Wisconsin State math standards or continue with the ACT skill bands. This allowed the team to disrupt the assertion that "not all students are Algebra ready" and instead focus on the adult work for selecting and implementing an improved, aligned, guaranteed, and viable curriculum.

This process is powerful. Again, our tendency is to jump to a solution without truly understanding the problem. Also, our tendency is to jump to an assertion that shifts responsibility from us to someone else, such as asserting that "not all students are Algebra ready."

Casey facilitated improvement conversations. The team determined the adjustments to make to address the problem. They applied actions to solve the problem and mapped out the solution. They trained people in the new approach to solidly execute the actions. And they continued to review their progress week after week by reviewing the data.

During the pandemic Casey continued to lead the academic teams of the School District of Menomonee Falls to apply improvement cycles. Even with the challenges of the pandemic, the school district achieved student learning gains over the two years. The operational departments in the school district also continued to achieve the goals, which became even more important during a time when schools had to enhance safety protocols. The school district improved and achieved positive results despite the obstacles the pandemic caused.

# Chapter 2 Summary

One of our partners, Waukesha County Government, Wisconsin, applies Principle 2 Measures that Matter with excellence. Dale Shaver, one of our Difference Maker Award recipients, presented at one of our conferences. His presentation was titled - *"It Takes More Than a Village: 4 Hospitals, a County Government and School Districts Mastermind Vaccinations for Schools."* Major strengths of his team are using data to define problems, aligning key actions to solve the problems, and tracking progress metrics to make needed adjustments to achieve goals. During the pandemic, they relied on these strengths to support 16 school districts in Waukesha County. At the onset of their work, his team discovered that the community was experiencing about 10-20 positive Covid cases a day, they had 75,000 K-12 students suddenly in new learning environments, unemployment skyrocketed from 2.3% to 11.7%, and over 18,500 people were suddenly newly unemployed.

Dale's team had developed strong relationships and a high level of trust with the Waukesha community. Over the years, they have provided excellent customer service. They constantly focused on using measures and data to improve their services. The Waukesha County Government team believed they could help the Waukesha schools and community manage the pandemic. They engaged in a successful approach to address the problems identified above.

Dale and his team deployed a "Unified Command Lead" working closely with the County Executive and Cabinet, Public Health, Emergency Management, and a Public Information Officer. Dale led teams including Contact Tracing, Education, Data Management, Testing, and Vaccinations. The teams determined key measures to monitor and constantly shared the information with community agencies, healthcare organizations and school districts. Here's one example of how Dale's team supported the community. They held weekly coordination and sharing meetings with 16 superintendents to develop and tweak protocols, create public messaging, and share support from businesses. Their goal was to provide a way for students to safely attend school in person. They believed that by achieving this goal, they could help the county reduce the unemployment rate. Rather than 16 school districts working alone, the county government brought the superintendents to a common table to work on one solution to support getting students back in school.

At the weekly meetings, the team convened 65 school nurses to review the number of school related Covid cases. The team also developed contact tracing protocols to track data in an expedited way to share with superintendents and the community.

Data-driven decisions made with real-time data, use of dashboards, and a constant reliance on consistent standards of excellence drove their success to accomplish the goal. By reviewing the measures, the team learned that with proper protocols, schools were safe for children and teachers. Of the 75,000 students attending in-person classes only 1% tested positive and of the positive cases, less than 1% of those were attributed to in-school transmission. There were no in-school transmissions between separate classroom cohorts, and less than .05% of students who were quarantined as direct contacts tested positive for COVID. Unemployment dropped from 11.7% to 3.5% and 18,500 unemployed residents dropped to 4,500 unemployed residents.

The Waukesha County Government measured what mattered to get students back in school and lower the unemployment rate in the community. They brought 16 school district leaders together to work on a common solution while assuming the role of tracking the most important measures to get students back to school and families to work. This team made a significant difference in their community.

Dale and his team are great models of how municipal governments serve their citizens. They measure what matters, determine key problems to solve, and align actions to achieve positive results. The team tracks data to provide the highest level of customer service to their community.

Principle 2 keeps leaders on track, focuses them on the right work, and makes them continuously aware of where to improve. The execution and improvement approach outlined is an iterative and continuous process that answers these questions.

- What are we trying to accomplish?
- What results are we trying to achieve?
- How do we systematically review where we are so that we know what to keep doing, stop doing, and adjust what we are doing?
- What changes can we make that will result in improvements?
- How do we apply a system to systematically review how we are doing in areas that are most critical to organizational success?

Our ability to execute through an improvement approach creates a path toward organizational excellence. Here's the good news. When we hardwire an execution and improvement approach in our organizations, we improve regardless of difficulties and uncertainties that appear. The mindset of our people is purposeful, and results driven. Our workplace culture becomes a place where we focus on the right things throughout the entire organization to offer an excellent student experience. We shift the difficulties to opportunities and hardwire improvement practices that make us better at getting better, never being satisfied and always striving for excellence.

As described in this chapter, we partner with educational leaders to hardwire Principle 2 as a key element for moving strategy to execution. Leaders create a district scorecard, track progress measures, engage in improvement conversations to identify problems, determine the root causes of the problems, and apply solutions. The scorecard process is an evidence-based leadership practice that reinforces the continuous search for improvement.

The process doesn't have to start at the district level only. A school or department can create their unit scorecards to drive the right team behaviors. We all want the highest student achievement, the best workplace environment, excellent service, a safe place to work, and financial efficiency. The measures that matter direct what we are trying to achieve and a way to assess how well we are doing along the way.

# 3

# BUILD A CULTURE AROUND SERVICE

*Serve others with great care and concern.*

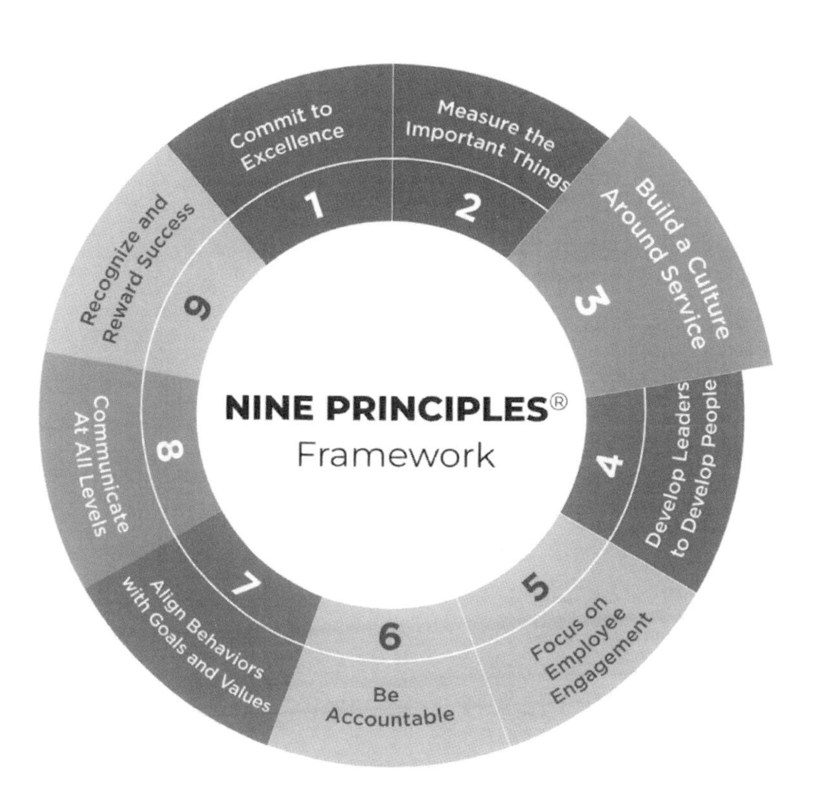

Providing excellent service to others is a must for educational organizations. Service is core to our mission. Our organizations cannot be excellent if we fail at service excellence. Building a culture around service must be part of our organizational DNA. Our goal is to ensure that the people we serve feel valued and receive positive outcomes. To achieve this goal, it's critical that we understand what people care about most. Chapter 3: Build a Culture Around Service focuses on people we serve, the value of feedback, service excellence surveys, service rounding, and service excellence tactics.

## Who We Serve and What They Expect

Who do we serve? We serve people we work with, those working directly with us and those who are part of the organization. We rely on our teams to provide great service. We serve students by ensuring that they have a positive experience and are safe from the time they are at the bus stop, in school during the day, and enjoying after-school activities. And we serve their families who come to us with varying degrees of needs. What's constant is that most families want what is best for their children. When we reach out to understand what that means and how we can collectively work for the best interest of their child, we focus on what matters.

In Chapter 1, Principle 1 Commit to Excellence, we summarized how to operationalize values by creating Standards of Excellence that serve as the backbone for providing great service. We use these standards to train employees in how to make service excellence a key component of our continuous improvement process. We can't be an excellent organization without providing excellent service.

The perceptions of most any profession fluctuate. Our goal in education is to keep a consistent positive image. Principle 3 Build a Culture Around Service helps us do just that. We put serving others as our highest priority, and it starts at the top. Senior leaders model service excellence for employees and recognize employees who serve others well.

As "customers" we expect to receive excellent service. See if these expectations resonate with you when you are a "customer." You want

- to feel valued and appreciated.
- people to listen to you and hear what you are saying.
- help from people who have a positive attitude and a desire to help.
- people to recognize that you have a problem.
- timely service rather than to be kept waiting and wondering.
- solutions that last rather than keep facing the same problem over and over again.
- people to address the problem rather than make excuses for why the problem is occurring.

On our Studer Education Team, providing the highest level of service to everyone we encounter is an ALWAYS Action. Amazing Service is one of our Studer Education team's Standards of Excellence. Annually, we hold several conferences and seminars. I start the conference with a welcome, reassuring our attendees that they are our special guests, and that our job is to provide the highest level of service. We want to provide them with a "10 out of 10" conference experience. Our conference team commits and acts to achieve this goal. Every detail is important. That's something that is extremely important to me. We practice the details before our guests arrive. When we miss, we are quick to call out the missteps and correct them as quickly as possible. Our conference performance represents who we are and how committed we are to people who give their precious time to be at the event.

Principle 3, Build a Culture Around Service requires leaders to develop themselves and their teams to provide outstanding service. We must work at building this culture by hardwiring key tools and tactics, some of which are provided in this chapter.

## Feedback is a Gift

A highlight during the springtime in Pensacola is opening the baseball season with the Blue Wahoos, a Double A affiliate with the Florida Marlins. Opening the season is hard work for employees, and sometimes mistakes are made. It can be difficult to get the season off to an exceptional start when you have a mix of new and experienced employees. The Blue Wahoos have a hardwired system, and even so, there are some mishaps. That sounds like a familiar story to us when we open a new school year. That opening sets the stage for the way we serve our staff, students, and their families.

Back to the Blue Wahoos story. Quint Studer who co-owns the Wahoos brought baseball to Pensacola 20 years ago. He was the owner of an Independent League Baseball team called the Pensacola Pelicans. I was a long-standing season ticket holder for the Pelicans. We played at the local university baseball stadium and had our core group of highly committed fans. It was a fun time – not much pitching to brag about. The games would end with a score like 14 to 10.

When Quint sold the Pelicans and bought a Double A team, the Wahoos, he let the season ticket holders have first choice of seats at the Wahoos stadium. It is a new stadium overlooking Pensacola Bay – it's drop dead gorgeous. All to say – I have good seats and in a section with many loyal fans.

At the end of a game the fans receive an online survey to complete asking them to rate their experience at the game. After the second game of the year, I received a survey. My experience that night had been below my expectations, which was highly unusual. I shared that information in the post-game survey. Specifically, I wrote this comment, *"Need to help employees develop. I know it's the first week yet have to train people to start strong. Great intentions by employees, Marginal training."* I come to games with high expectations because of the consistency and commitment to service excellence by the Wahoos throughout the years.

Donna Kirby, the leader of service excellence, sent the following email to me at 9:56 AM, the morning after I completed the survey. She copied Quint Studer and the President of the Blue Wahoos. Quint sent me a note thanking me for my input as Donna connected with me. Here is Donna's email to me.

*Hi, Janet:*

*Thank you for coming out to see some Blue Wahoos baseball, and for taking the time to give us feedback on your survey.*

*I noticed that you rated someone on our team as "poor," and I was hoping you could give me a little insight into what drove that rating, please. This team member reports to me, so any specifics about the situation you are able to provide can be used as valuable training for my whole staff. Additionally, in your comment you noted "marginal training." I was hoping you could expand on that a little more, so I have a better understanding of exactly which areas you noticed are lacking. Any feedback you can provide would certainly be helpful – thank you!*

*We hope to see you back at another Blue Wahoos game soon, Janet.*

*Thank you and have a great day!*

After I received her email, Donna's genuine tone motivated me to respond with the same line of respect. Her approach helped me provide better feedback. I wanted to provide feedback so that employees could be successful. And she highlighted some areas she wanted to learn more about. She guided my response with her tone and choice of words. I knew I needed to be thoughtful because she would apply the information if she found it helpful.

Here's my response back:

*Hello Donna,*

*Thank you for reaching out. Some positive feedback along with some information.*

1. *Bob was with us in our section on the first night and he is always great - This year and last year. He is welcoming, friendly, proactive with fans, and serves people without being asked. Bob wasn't there last night and the individual in our section did not do any-*

*thing in particular except I did not find him engaged because of the way I've had encounters with some fantastic people throughout the years.*

2. *My comment about training aligned more with concessions. Very nice interactions with people there; yet, not very professional for what you most likely want to see. I ordered fish and fries. Three people behind me ordered – one person fish and fries, one person fries, and one person corn dog and fries. I was ordering during the top of the 7th inning. We had to wait on fries (which is fine). The person behind me received fish and fries first, then the person received fries, then there was a chicken finger dinner that came out that no one ordered. The re-order of corn dogs with fries occurred and took priority over my order. I was left standing. And, then the message that I had to wait on fries again. I like to watch the game, missed Wahoos scoring, and then in a very nice way, the individual mentioned to me that I could watch the replay on the big screen. I left wondering, what would happen if they were busy? It seemed more like a training issue than employees' desire to do the right work. Because they were very nice, I almost ignored providing feedback. That would not be fair to them, so I completed the survey. And most of the time I complete with very positive ratings. I love the games and want the Wahoos to be the best.*
3. *I appreciate you personally making an effort to connect with several loyal fans in our section last night. As a leader, I use you as an example of a model high performer. In fact, I recognized you in one of my weekly podcast episodes.*

*Thank you for asking.*

*Janet*

Here's Donna's response back to me:

*Thank you so much, Janet, for all of your enormously helpful feedback. Incident-driven information, where I can highlight specifics, always seems to "stick better" when I'm coaching my team so thank you!*

*We had someone who was new to our team fill in for Bob. He is new to the team and has been through all of our pre-season training but was so nervous that he was unable to hit the mark in that role last night. Being a newbie, I should've placed him elsewhere and put someone more experienced in that particular location. This is a lesson for me, so thank you for bringing it to my attention. Good news is that Bob is back tonight! I agree with you – he's the best! Did you know that he's a retired Marine Corps Commandant? At one time, he oversaw over 1,000 direct reports and was a leader of the USMC Merchant Marine Academy. An impressive person whom I'm happy to have on our Blue Wahoos staff.*

*Janet, I'm adding Eric, our GM of Food & Beverage, onto this email chain so that he can see your feedback about your experience at the concessions. You may remember Eric from prior seasons when he was a member of our inaugural season Blue Wahoos team. Eric understands the world class experience we want for each of our fans, so your feedback will help him coach his team on process, procedures and communications.*

*Lastly, I am humbled by your very kind words, and to have been included on your podcast - thank you! I am fortunate to be able to do something I love for a cause that I truly believe in. If I can ever be of service to you, please let me know.*

*In the meantime, we are going to get busy with coaching from your feedback. Again, I appreciate your time and effort, Janet. Hope to get to see you at another Blue Wahoos game SOON!*

Wow! This is an ideal example of providing excellent service. Let's review several of the stellar service recovery actions.

1. Donna thanked me for providing specific, incident focused feedback so she would know how to coach an employee.
2. She took responsibility for making a placement error with a new, inexperienced team member and did not place the blame on the employee. The employee was new and nervous, and she placed the employee in the section with the most loyal fans. No wonder he was nervous. I would have been as well if in his shoes.
3. She reinforced my recognition of Bob by making sure I knew his credentials. She managed up Bob to give him even more credibility. Wouldn't you want a boss like Donna? I know I sure would.
4. She connected me with Eric, the leader of concessions, and promoted his skill set. She let me know how committed he was to his work and team, and she reminded me that I know him from his time in another role with the Wahoos.
5. She appreciated the recognition I gave to her and topped it off with how grateful she is to do work that she loves.
6. She continued to offer her services to me.

I am confident Donna cares about me having an excellent experience. She values me as a fan. That's unforgettable service. As I'm doing here, I will keep telling this story again and again.

That's why feedback is a gift. It builds customer loyalty. It helps us improve, gives us opportunities to develop people to improve their performance, and offers information to recognize people for good performance and behavior.

We want to delight the people we serve. People expect encounters to be timely, accurate, and friendly. Going beyond expectations brings a delightful experience. People tell others about the experience. I travel to Chicago several times a year. I am a Marriott Rewards member and choose to stay with that chain most of the time. In Chicago I typically stay at the Marriott property - Sheraton Grand Chicago Riverwalk Hotel. During the Fall of 2021 the hotel was working to come back online after COVID. I decided to have dinner in the hotel restaurant. Only the bar area was open with a limited menu. I sat at the bar. The bartender introduced himself and provided tremendous service. He made me feel special. I learned that he had worked at the hotel for over 20 years. The leadership of the hotel kept him on even when they were losing money from COVID. He was appreciative. When I left that evening, I had even more loyalty to the Marriott brand. When I returned on my next trip, I chose to go to the bar to eat dinner so that I could see the bartender who gave me delightful service. He remembered me. Now, that's great service from leadership to the frontline staff. The bottom line is all employees and leaders are responsible for service excellence.

Sometimes customer service is reactive. We wait for someone to complain about issues before we try to resolve them. Of course, we offer to help people when there are problems. Our goal, however, is to identify potential problems proactively before they occur, allowing us to address issues before someone encounters a problem with our service. By anticipating customer needs, we demonstrate a deeper understanding of who our customers are and what they need. Our proactive and positive actions build their trust with us. Over time, they are loyal to our organization.

A culture of service excellence depends on feedback we receive from those we serve so that we can anticipate and solve potential problems. It also depends on consistently applying service excellence tactics associated with communicating effectively. Let's focus on the areas to hardwire in our organizations to be proactive with our approach to service excellence.

## Service Excellence Surveys and Roll Out Process

To gain insight from our internal and external customers, our team administers service surveys, provides results reports, and develops leaders to roll out the results. The roll out process includes leaders sharing results with the participants and engaging in conversations about the meaning of the results. The conversation ultimately leads to an improvement action.

Many educational organizations use feedback surveys. Regardless of the type of survey administered, it has little value if leaders fail to share and act on the results. At times, we hear people say that surveys are not useful tools. That's true when we conduct a survey and fail to do something with the results. People who take valuable time to complete the survey deserve to see the results and improvement actions taken. Sharing encourages people to complete the surveys in meaningful ways. The value of the survey comes from what we do with the data to help us improve. The goal is to gather information, review the results, share the results, and create improvement actions.

Let's look at some of the surveys our team uses with leaders to gain feedback from those they serve.

*Student Surveys*

Students come to school each day choosing whether to be engaged learners or not. Gathering student success data is important to understand if our students are progressing. We also want to know how they are feeling about their learning environment. Surveying our students from time to time provides us with aggregate information we can share with students. We learn what's working well and where students are struggling in their classes. We can also evaluate how engaged and safe they feel at school and how connected they feel to their teacher and their peers.

To gain feedback from students, we administer our Student Engagement Survey and train leaders and teachers to roll out the results. The school gets an overall results report. The results are rolled out by following a process to share results and gain input.

- The principal rolls out the results to teachers sharing areas working well and where improvements need to occur.
- Teachers roll out the results to students and gain their insight. That information can be shared with other grade level teachers. Information from the roll out sessions with students is shared with the principal.
- The principal works with the school staff to create one to three improvement actions to focus on at the school.

- Working with teachers, the principal creates a way for the information to be communicated to parents.
- Finally, all principals share their learnings from the roll out session with the district office.

The feedback is used to celebrate the bright spots and determine the one to three improvement actions that can be applied in the school. Remember the rule of thumb for selecting the number of actions to work on at one time. If we select one to three actions, we have an opportunity to achieve the goals. Selecting more than three actions reduces our odds.

*Family Surveys*

It's important to gain insight from families. Families are asked about their level of satisfaction with their child's learning experience. The goal for gathering feedback is to determine areas working well and needing improvements.

Families are given an opportunity to take the Family/Parent Satisfaction Survey. The school gets an overall results report. Like the student surveys, the results are rolled out by following a process to share results and gain input.

- The principal rolls out the results to teachers sharing what's working well and where improvements need to occur.
- The principal works with the school staff to create one to three improvement actions to focus on at the school.
- Working with teachers, the principal creates a way for the information to be communicated to families.
- Finally, all principals share their learnings from the roll out session with the district office.

*Support Service Excellence Survey*

Our educational departments also provide services to teams within our schools and departments. We administer a Support Service Excellence Survey. This survey is intended for key leaders of the organization to provide input to other leaders about internal services. Leaders have an opportunity to provide helpful information that department leaders can use to continuously improve. Most departmental employees want to do a good job. Giving constructive feedback helps them do their jobs better.

Selected leaders are given an opportunity to take the Support Service Excellence Survey. The departments get a results report and roll them out to their teams and the leaders by following a defined process.

- The department leader rolls out the results to departmental employees sharing what's working well and where improvements need to occur.
- The conversations lead to determining one to three improvement actions to focus on.
- The department leader shares the improvement actions with other organizational leaders continuing to ask for feedback on ways the department is improving.
- Finally, all department leaders share their learnings from the roll out session with key organizational leaders.

It's important to note that the size of the organization directs the way information needs to be cascaded. We've used our surveys with educational systems or with subsets of systems - a school or department. The key to the survey process is administering surveys to gather feedback, reviewing the results to determine what's working and what's not, sharing the results with others, engaging in meaningful conversations about the results, and applying improvement actions to work on.

As we apply the improvement actions, it's important to report to the groups surveyed the actions we are taking, and the progress being made. Doing so helps the survey respondents recognize that we value their input. We can probe for deeper understanding by applying service rounds with those we serve.

## Service Rounding

One way to gain insights proactively from people in a more comprehensive way is to round with people we serve. Rounding conversations are one-on-one connections with people. We round with people for various reasons. We learn what's working well, what processes can be improved, and who needs to be recognized for good performance or behavior. General rounding questions are

- What's working well?
- What's getting in the way of you doing your best?
- Is there anyone who has been especially helpful to you? What did they do?
- What can I do to be helpful to you?

These questions can be tailored to the type of rounding we do with various audiences and purposes. We may round with students and their families. To follow-up on the internal Support Service Excellence Survey department leaders may round with individuals who use their services. Let's look at several examples.

- *Student Rounding.* Let's say, in class we've implemented a new way to do small group work.

Our goal is to get students more engaged and feel a sense of belonging in class. Teachers may choose to round with a handful of students asking,

- What's working well with our new small group structure? What do you like about it?
- What's getting in the way of you being able to learn in your small group?
- Are there students who have been helpful to make the new small group structure work? What did they do?
- What can I do to be helpful to you and other students when we are in small groups?

- *Family Rounding*. Let's say the principal at a middle school worked with a team of 6th grade teachers to create a process to round with a cross section of parents during the school's open house and at the car line where parents drop off and pick up their children from school. The teachers asked these questions during the rounding session,
    - What's working well with your child at school?
    - What's getting in the way of your child having a great experience at school?
    - Is there anyone who has been especially helpful to you at the school? What did they do?
    - What can I do to be helpful to you and your child?

  One of the lowest scored items on the parent survey is "the school provides positive feedback about my child." Rounding with families can help school leaders and teachers know what families value about receiving positive feedback about their child. We train school leaders to apply a family rounding approach to gain input on how families want to receive that information. Principals train teachers to apply a structured approach asking families these questions.

  - When you've received positive feedback about your child, what did you like about it?
  - What ways would you like to receive positive feedback about your child? What type of information would you like to hear?
  - Is there a teacher that's provided positive feedback to you and that you think has done that well? What did they do?

- *Department Service Rounding.* Using the Support Service Excellence Survey results as a catalyst for rounding helps leaders focus on specific processes to improve. For example, the IT department may have received lower scores on their timeliness to respond. It may be difficult for the IT staff to solve some of the problems that come to them in the ticket system in a timely way. They want to know how they could do a better job when that occurs. The leader of the IT Department rounds with other leaders to gain input by asking,
  - We are trying to improve our timeliness in our IT department. When we are doing that well, what are we doing?
  - When we are not being timely with our response, what's not working?
  - Do you have suggestions on what we can do to be helpful to you when we can't solve the problem right away?
  - Is there anyone on our IT team that has been especially helpful or someone who is timely with responses? What did they do?

Service rounding with others takes little time yet produces huge returns. Rounding helps us build positive relationships with those we serve. It informs us about the good work being done, what is being done, and how we can apply the best practice on our team. Finally, rounding lets people know we care about providing excellent service.

Dan Buryj is the Vice President of Administration and Finance at Coker University, South Carolina. Dr. Natalie Harder, the Coker University President, hired Dan to make modifications to strengthen the division. His department administered the support service excellence survey to get baseline information. He used that information to do service rounds with other leaders at the university to guide him on ways to make changes. Dan shared the information with his team and applied improvement actions. A year later, he improved his scores in every category. The overall score increased by 0.70!! Placing service excellence as a key priority produced amazing service delivery by the finance and administration team.

| | BASELINE MEAN | ONE YEAR |
|---|---|---|
| Service Delivery | 3.44 | 4.07 |
| Customer Focused | 3.37 | 4.11 |
| Positive Interactions | 3.51 | 4.14 |
| Solutions Focused | 3.28 | 4.00 |
| Helping Attitude | 3.28 | 4.09 |
| **Overall** | **3.38** | **4.08** |

I was in a meeting where we shared the results with Dan and the executive team. His colleagues spoke about Dan and his team rounding and using feedback to make meaningful changes in the department. Dan and his team shared improvement actions with people in the organization, they improved the way they followed up on projects and services, and they explained why decisions were made. Dan's colleagues mentioned that rather than giving a no answer to requests, Dan and his team would say *"we can't do that, but what if we try this."* They came up with alternatives to try to reach good solutions. Within a year these seemingly small actions produced unbelievably improved results. Dan and his team invested their time to act on the feedback and make connections with others to improve their services. It was made possible by a strong President who believes in providing the best service to students, families, faculty, staff and the community.

## Key Service Excellence Tactics

Customer service is a point of pride in the way we serve our students, families, and employees. Education is a service-focused profession. Thus, we must be the best at providing excellent service. To do so, it's important to develop leaders and employees on key service excellence tactics.

Service excellence is determined by how our "customers" perceive us. We want people we serve to feel a sense of loyalty to our organization. We use a Net Promoter Score (NPS) measure for assessing student, family, and employee perceptions on how likely they are to recommend our schools and districts to others. The Net Promoter Score gives us a number we can compile and track regularly and benchmark to other educational organizations and industries. The NPS score helps us measure what's core to our bottom line – that people we serve trust that we are providing the best educational experience for our students and families.

Developing our leaders and staff to consistently apply key service excellence tactics is essential to this bottom line. Some organizations mistakenly believe service training is only for staff. Providing excellent service is everyone's responsibility. Therefore, we recommend organizations provide service excellence training to everyone.

We've hired leader coaches who are retired from their superintendent positions and have partnered with our team. These former superintendents, Dr. Pat Greco, Dr. DeDe Ashby, and Tim Wyrosdick, sat in the room and participated during their school district training sessions and engaged as a participant with their employees. We see this occurring throughout the country with our partner organizations. Service excellence starts at the top and is everyone's job.

So far, we've described the survey roll out process and service rounding. In this section, I summarize key service excellence tactics to standardize in your organizations. These tactics provide simple, powerful, and quick ways to positively shift the culture of an organization.

*The 5/10 Rule*

Service Excellence means never having anyone feel ignored. Here's a practice to hardwire with everyone in your organization. When people are 10 feet away from us, gesture a greeting with eye contact, a head nod, wave, or smile. As they approach us and are 5 feet away, greet them by saying hello, nice to see you, or how are you doing today. This simple tactic makes people feel welcome.

Someone asked me the other day, what if the person has their head down or has their earbuds in their ears. I responded – do it anyway. I work with higher education institutions as part of my coaching work. To get from one place to another, I usually walk across campus. I make sure I greet every student I see in this way. Typically, about one-half of the students respond to my greetings. It's great to get a smile back from a student. Maybe that student will remember how welcoming the 5/10 greeting felt and pass it on to someone else. Applying the 5/10 Rule takes no additional time, and very little energy. We feel good and can help someone else feel like they matter.

*60-Second Rule*

Sixty seconds is a long time to wait to be greeted as a customer, especially if service providers appear to be busy with other things (on the phone, typing on the computer, talking to another employee). The 60-Second Rule means that everyone is greeted and acknowledged within 60 seconds of entering a space, even if everyone is busy. Within 60 seconds, we make eye contact with the customer, let them know that we see them, and communicate that we will serve them as soon as possible.

Sometimes people ask, *"What if employees do this and the greeting isn't genuine?"* I respond – being genuine is something we must do. If we have push back in this way, we've got a problem with people not following the Standards of Excellence. That's why the standards are so important to develop right out of the gate and part of Principle 1 Commit to Excellence. Here's what typically occurs. We start by making the 5/10 Rule and the 60-Second Rule mandatory. By doing the actions, employees start feeling better about themselves and how they are treating others. They understand why doing these simple, yet powerful tactics begins to build a better culture. The odds are the person applying the 60-Second Rule will get positive interactions from customers. Isn't that better than living in negativity?

I travel often. From time to time, I go to the hotel counter for assistance. It seems that about 30% of the time the hair dryer has gone missing in my room. That's a must have for me. In one instance when this occurred, I eagerly approached the counter to solve my dilemma. The front desk employee was doing some paperwork. I took a step back to honor that she was busy. A couple of minutes passed by. Now I am getting antsy because I'm on my way to a meeting. I thought if only she would apply the 60-second rule, my anxiety would be reduced. At least I would know she saw me standing in front of her. At some point she finally asked if she could help me. She said that I would have a hair dryer in my room by the end of the day. All day, I debated if I should stop by the CVS down the street on my way back from my partner visit and buy a hair dryer or trust there would be one in my room. Late that afternoon, I went to my room and found the hair dryer on the bathroom counter. Here's the point – my anxiety lasted the entire day because I did not have confidence that the service provider would solve a problem that was important to me. Great service means we proactively act to reduce others' anxiety. We want people to depend on us and trust that we will help them.

The 5/10 and 60-second rules are easy to apply and powerful to build customer connections. Also, doing a little homework prior to the day can go a long way. I also stay in the same hotels when I go to visit clients. I may stay at the same hotel 6 to 8 times a year in a city. Over the past decade, I've only had one person greet me by my name every time I stayed at the hotel. He was promoted to a manager's position and left the hotel. That was good for him and bad for the hotel. My experience changed, and I chose a different hotel to align to the brand I am most loyal to. Small things make a big difference.

*AIAE (Acknowledge, Introduce, Ask, Ensure, or Escort)*

A standard informational greeting starts a customer encounter off in the right way. We follow this protocol to start a conversation with a customer.

- **A**cknowledge the customer.
- **I**ntroduce ourselves.
- **A**sk what we can do to help them.
- **E**nsure them we will help them or escort them to a place where they can receive help.

Here's an example message. *"Hello - I am Audrey, the office assistant. What can I do to help you today? Yes- I can help you find Mr. Smith's office. Let me walk you there."* Sometimes the customer will respond in this way. *"Oh- you don't have to do that. I can get there if you point the way"* Here's what we recommend as your response. *"It's no problem at all. I would enjoy walking with you."* The high impact of this experience comes from that standard informational greeting and the follow through that makes the "customer" feel special. If you can't walk them to the place, provide them with directions and give them your contact information in case they get lost. When someone asks for help, you own ensuring they receive the best service, even if you are not the person to help them get to the outcome they desire.

*AIDET (Acknowledge, Introduce, Duration, Explain, Thank)*

At times, we are performing a particular service for a customer where we want the customer to have confidence in our services. They need to know more details about the service process. Our goal is to educate them on what will occur and to reduce their anxiety about the specifics of the service. Let's say someone comes to the Human Resources

Office inquiring about positions in the organization. The person is nervous and not clear about what to do. The HR Specialist greets the individual and uses AIDET to reduce the person's anxiety about being there and asking for help.

- **A (Acknowledge):** Hello. We are glad you are here.
- **I (Introduce):** I am Jennifer, an HR Specialist with the district. My role is to help people who inquire about job openings.
- **D (Duration):** We have an initial process we use to explain the job application process. It will take about 20 to 30 minutes to work through this process. If you have time, I will be glad to work with you now.
- **E (Explanation):** There are several steps in the job application process. During this first step, I will gain clarity on the positions you are interested in, go over the application process, recommend the next steps, and answer questions you have.
- **T (Thank You):** I appreciate the opportunity to work with you and your interest in our district.

*Voice Mail Messages*

Here are 5 elements for creating a voice mail message that demonstrates excellent service. The person on the voice mail

- starts with a welcome hello.
- identifies who they are and the department that's been contacted.
- summarizes what to do to get service by leaving the caller's name, contact information, and the information needed from the office.
- provides the time expectation for returning calls such as the caller can expect a return call within 48 hours.

- closes the call thanking the caller and acknowledging that we look forward to serving them soon.

*Out of Office Email Message*

Like voice mail messages, we also create out of office email messages that tell customers a great deal about the commitment level to be good service providers. Here are 3 elements that are critical when creating an out-of-office email reply that will meet the needs of customers.

- First, thank them for the message and state the expected state of return. You could write - *Thank you for your email. I will return to the office on Friday, January 3rd and answer your email then.*
- Second, ask the person connecting with you to leave information about the service needed so you can work on the need prior to connecting with them. You could write - *Please let me know the nature of the service I can provide to you, what information you need, or what issues we need to discuss so I can be ready to assist you quickly upon my return.*
- Third, provide a team member's contact information in case of a time-sensitive issue that can't wait until your return. You could write - *If your service request is urgent, please reach out to Lindsay Lewis at 285-759-0090 or email her at llewis@customerservice.com.*

*Successful Handovers*

At times, we need to shift the "customer" to someone else to help them. For example, a "customer" could contact you when they clearly need to be in contact with another department. Or, we may have a personnel transition causing us to shift service from one person to another. Here's how we manage handovers.

Never let them know that they are in the wrong place or with the wrong person. Instead, listen to the issue or need, explain that the "expert" in that area is one of your colleagues and proactively connect the customer with your colleague by phone or written correspondence. If in person, escort the person to the right office. Along the way, take the opportunity to position your colleague well. You might say -*You are in good hands with Mr. Morales. He is experienced and always tries to find the best solution to meet people's needs.*

*Dealing with Difficult Customers*

You may be asking, what do we do if someone is difficult to work with or angry? Start with diffusing a person's anger.

- Stay calm and understand that this is not personal. Most likely they are not upset with you; they are upset with the situation.
- Listen, without interruption. They need someone to hear their story. After you give them a chance to speak, get and use their name. You may say something like, *what did you say your name was*?
- Actively sympathize by acknowledging their distress. You can say, *I can see this has certainly upset you.*
- These three actions treat people with respect and show that you want to understand them and their issues. Now apply actions that move to solutions.
- Apologize with grace. You are not taking blame. You are apologizing for what has upset them.
- Begin to work toward a solution. Include them in the discussion of the best solution. At times we can

solve the problem on the spot. At other times, we need to take the next step to get closer to a solution.

- Work with them to come to an agreement on the next steps to solve their issue or to move closer to resolution. If there are additional steps, ensure that you or someone on your team will follow up with them to make sure they are getting the assistance needed.
- Finally, take care of you by giving yourself time to collect your thoughts and feelings. Remember, the problem is seldom with you. In fact, after you go through the steps presented, the customer may even feel good about you and how you are helping them.

One last note. If the customer is being extremely difficult and threatening, these steps may not diffuse the situation. You may need to shift away from the situation and communicate the occurrence to your leader. If a situation is toxic and a person is irrational, there's not much we can do to help until the person has an opportunity to calm down. You may say something like this – *I am sorry that you are so upset. I am willing to work through your issue when we can move toward identifying and solving the problem at hand. When you are prepared to work through the problem, please feel free to contact me to work on the problem.* Put the action back in the hands of the person acting irrationally. If you put the action on you and you fail to follow-up, the customer has even more reason to be mad.

*Service Recovery*

We are not perfect. We'll make mistakes from time to time. Therefore, we need a good service recovery process to address these mistakes. The first thing we do is own the mistake with those who are receiving our services. Work to understand the error from the customers' view and gain clarity on what they see as the right action on our part to correct the error. Never try to blame others or excuse away the error. Accept and acknowledge that we have delivered services that are not up to our standard. Apologize with sincerity and gain insight into the problem so we can fix it. Then, take action to solve the problem and follow up with the customer to ensure that the correct action has been taken. The story about Donna Kirby on the opening week of the Blue Wahoos season is an excellent example of how to apply service recovery when you make mistakes.

Sometimes our customers are our employees. We've all experienced two team members being against each other needing to do service recovery with each other. As a supervisor, it's our job to help manage this conflict by addressing it head on. Here's what I've found works. Once the two individuals have reached a rational state, ask them to meet with you. Provide some ground rules for the discussion, such as being respectful of other participants, not interrupting others, sticking to the topic, and listening with an open mind. Then guide the discussion between the two team members to get to a positive outcome. We rarely take this action; rather we avoid the issues and hope the situation improves over time. That seldom occurs. In fact, the damaged relationship usually escalates to a more severe level. The sooner we address conflict with internal and external customers, the better able we are to solve the problem.

## Chapter 3 Summary

The tried-and-true tools and tactics in this chapter build a culture of service excellence. They work well when leaders and staff consistently deploy the tactics. It's important then to train and develop people in the tactics and create a process for ensuring that leaders and staff are applying service excellence practices.

To be an excellent organization, building a culture around service is a key commitment by leaders. The tactics presented in this chapter are foundational actions for everyone to practice. Every person in the organization applies service excellence tactics every day, all the time.

In the first year of our partnership, Burton School District in California committed to training all leaders and employees on the key service excellence tactics. They also continued to train their leaders on service rounding as well as most all tools and tactics in this book. The Burton leaders administered the surveys described in this chapter and applied a survey roll out process to build improvement action plans for the district, departments, and schools. Superintendent Sergio Mendoza and his leadership team place a high priority on service, and they work at hardwiring the nine principles tools and tactics to create actions that always occur. Subsequently, students, families, and employees feel their perceptions count and that they are treated with the highest level of respect.

Superintendent Mendoza is deeply committed to being a premier school district. He is one of our first partner districts to apply the continuous improvement process from the boardroom to the classroom. What makes Burton School District so special is they place service excellence as the cornerstone of being an excellent organization. Superintendent Mendoza refers to these words by Mahatma Gandhi, *"The customer is the most important visitor on our premises. He is not dependent on us. We are dependent on him. He is not an interruption of our work. He is the purpose of it. He is not an outsider of our business. He is part of it. We are not doing him a favor by serving him. He is doing us a favor by giving us the opportunity to do so."*

I've had an opportunity to visit the Burton School District. As I walked in the administrative building, I was greeted with a warm welcome feeling like I was a special guest. I experienced "10 out of 10" service with Burton employees. It's an experience I will always remember, I am grateful to this team for putting the service excellence tactics into action to serve the Burton School District community.

Service excellence is far reaching. It extends beyond our organizations to the communities we serve. In our communities, we are at our best when we share a mutual concern for each other's well-being. The pandemic presented challenging issues in our communities that pulled us in opposing directions. Our educational institutions have relied on providing excellent service to help them navigate the rough waters.

While some tragic events tear us apart, others bring us together if we are truly committed to serving others. During the pandemic years, we witnessed several of our partner organizations experiencing disasters including fires, earthquakes, hurricanes, tornadoes, and shootings. I am struck by how the organizational leaders relied on the foundational tools and tactics in this book to manage through tremendous change.

I'm also struck by how strong the leaders feel about their communities. Two of our Louisiana Gulf Coast community colleges experienced extreme damage from weather events. Fletcher Technical and Community College took a direct hit from Hurricane Ian that devastated the entire community and caused severe structural damage to part of the college campus. Nunez Community College, still recovering from a direct hit from Hurricane Katrina in 2005, also had damage from subsequent Gulf Coast hurricanes. Nunez also experienced damage from tornadoes that touched down in the same location occurring within 9 months of each other.

Both college Chancellor's Dr. Kristine Strickland (Chancellor of Fletcher Technical and Community College) and Dr. Tina Tinney (Chancellor of Nunez Community College) were making difficult decisions to position their institutions for the future when the natural disasters occurred. They could have easily placed the work on hold, but they chose to continue with the changes that they knew were in the best interest of the college, students, and their respective communities. They continued to do the difficult work and serve their communities to get people back on their feet and students back in school.

Here's what is even more impressive about their leadership. We hold quarterly strategy retreats with higher education institutions we work with. The summer following Hurricane Ian, the two leaders brought their executive teams together to meet with Dr. Julie Kunselman, one of our Studer Education coaches, and me in New Orleans. They opened their hearts and minds to learning from each other, helping each other, and doing the right work to serve their employees and communities. The executive leaders set an example for their leadership teams to engage in collaborative conversations about areas working well and those needing improvements. That day the two teams were serving each other. They've asked us to connect the two teams together once a year.

Principle 3 Build a Culture Around Service is core to our work with partner organizations. That's because to be a great organization, service excellence is a must have, not a nice to have. Superintendent Mendoza and Chancellors Strickland and Tinney place service to others above themselves.

# 4

# DEVELOP LEADERS TO DEVELOP PEOPLE

*Coach people to be at their best.*

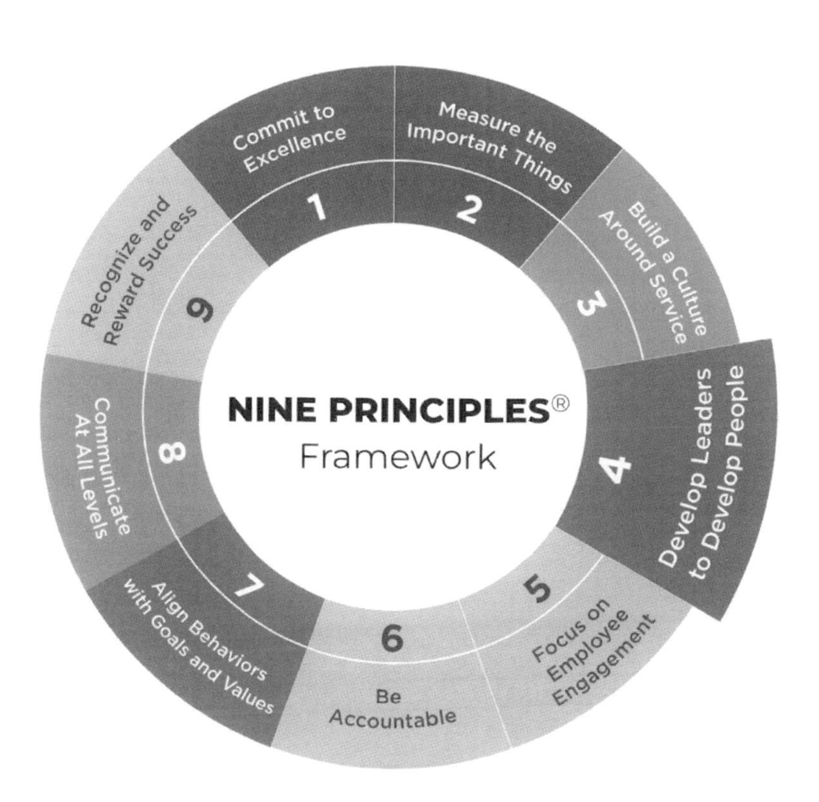

Excellent organizations have excellent leaders. Excellent leaders know that they haven't led well until their teams have performed well. They see that one of their top priorities is coaching people to be at their best. For people to be at their best, they need to work in an environment that supports their growth and development.

As I am writing this book, we are experiencing historical records of employee turnover in education, business, and industry. In education, we read articles that show alarming statistics about teachers and staff leaving the education profession. More than ever, we need leaders who are skilled at creating positive work environments. A leader is one of the biggest factors influencing whether employees stay or leave their positions.

According to a report by the Education Policy Institute, 90% of the teacher shortage demand comes from turnover. When we lose a teacher, it costs between $9,000 and $21,000 to replace a teacher (Learning Policy Institute). A study by the New Teachers Project almost a decade ago called the *Irreplaceables*, indicated that we have a 1 in 11 chance to hire a high performing teacher when a high performing teacher leaves. Those odds will factor against us every year unless we change the way we approach developing leaders. The research asserts that K12 leaders haven't lived the recommendations of this study to position us in a better place today. In essence, the study concluded that America's urban schools are taking a negligent approach to teacher retention. That is, leaders rarely make a strong effort to keep teachers who are successful at advancing student learning and being a contributing professional. Leaders are also unsuccessful with ushering out low performing teachers. In summary, the key findings are the following.

- Principals make far too little effort to retain "Irreplaceables" or remove low-performing teachers.
- Poor school cultures and working conditions drive away great teachers.
- Policies give principals and district leaders few incentives to change their ways.

To combat the retention crisis, we need to make keeping our highest performers a top priority, coaching good solid performers to improve, and addressing low performing teachers to improve or transition out of the profession.

What held true a decade ago, still holds true today. Some may say the political factors have a bigger play today. There will always be political factors that influence education. At times those factors are stronger than at other times. *Hardwiring Excellence in Education* focuses on factors we can control. Without question, Principle 4 Develop Leaders to Develop People is in our control.

People in education choose the profession because they have passion to support students to be successful. This purpose cuts across our educational organizations in both academic and operational areas. Our employees want to come to a place where they feel like they have purpose, do worthwhile work, and can make a difference. They want to feel part of things. And they want to be recognized and appreciated. Leaders hold the key to retaining good employees. It's important for organizations to get key leaders in the right seats and make leader development a high priority.

The first three principles set the stage for turning the flywheel. Whatever gains we get from the first 3 principles will not be sustained without making leader development a key priority. If we fail to develop leaders' skill sets, our leaders cannot succeed. We also demonstrate a lack of commitment to living our organizational values.

What makes Principle 4, Develop Leaders to Develop People so important?

I've had conversations with leaders about employee turnover. They ask what some of our partner organizations are doing to reduce turnover.

I respond, *"Investing in their people and developing their leaders to build great teams to solve difficult problems, consistently and constantly."*

*"How can I do that?"*

*"Make leader development one of the most critical actions in your organization. Make it a must do in your organization and mean it with your actions and commitment,"* I reply.

*"But where do I find time?"*

I respond, *"When you make leader development a mandatory practice for leaders in your organization, you will save time on problems you are spending time on now. You put continuous improvement and solution building front and center for everyone."*

Leader development can take shape in different ways. We can hold in person leadership development institutes, design a leadership development structure to engage in leadership development online, support leaders with coaches and mentors, and integrate leadership development as a key part of our leadership meeting agendas. Regardless of the approach, let's make leadership development one of our top priorities for hardwiring leadership essentials in our organizations.

## Essential Leadership Skills

In every chapter of this book, I focus on ways we can advance our leadership skills. I've found that there are essential leadership practices that are fundamental to our work: leader rounding, 30- and 90- day conversations, communication with key words, and reward and recognition. These tactics are outlined in more detail in subsequent chapters.

As we apply the Nine Principles Framework, we first and foremost want to create an "emotional bank account" with our teams. We all have a bank account where we make money deposits. At times we need to pay for something from our account, so we place enough money in the bank to be able to do so. The more we have in our account, the less stress we feel when we cash in.

Let's transfer this thinking from a money bank account to an emotional bank account. An emotional bank account is an account of trust – it's how safe people feel and how connected they are to others at work. The more we deposit emotional good into our account, the safer people feel when leaders must cash in.

For example, sometimes leaders need to share feedback with their direct reports to help them improve. A trusting relationship makes these types of conversations go much better. Even after 30 years and counting, I remember my first year of teaching high school. I had a mentor teacher and supervisor, Ms. Calley. She was a great teacher and an even greater mentor and supervisor. She observed me teaching in my classroom throughout the year. Prior to her observations, she reduced my anxiety by engaging in conversations with me. She said things like, *"I look forward to being in your classroom tomorrow. I am confident in you as a teacher and the relationships you have with your students in the classroom."*

When she gave me feedback about my teaching, she started with the positives and then gave me a pointer or two that would help me improve. After all the years gone by, I still remember my experiences with Ms. Calley like they were yesterday. She had the power and authority to influence if I stayed in the profession or left during my first year of teaching. Ms. Calley demonstrated fundamental leadership skills that made a difference in my life and in turn, the lives of my students. Teachers and staff members deserve leaders who build trusting relationships with them.

To be successful leaders, we need employees to be at their best. Leaders depend on their teams to achieve critical results. Employees depend on leaders to apply essential leadership skills to keep them focused and productive at work. They expect leaders to

- stay in tune with their needs.
- act in ways that show true care and concern for their well-being.
- invest in their growth and development.
- share quick wins and organizational bright spots.

- recognize and appreciate them for their contributions.
- remove existing barriers that get in the way of them doing their jobs.
- clearly communicate the direction of the organization.
- help them know what is expected of them.
- show them that their contributions matter.

It's easy to see that leaders need the right skills to lead their teams. Good leaders are always focused on ways they can improve. That's what this book is about. Every chapter includes essential leadership skills for achieving organizational excellence.

## Performance Curve

I now turn to outlining what leaders need to consider and be able to do to develop employees they supervise by reviewing the organizational performance curve (Figure 8). Decades of research indicate that people in our organizations, including leaders fall along a performance continuum. We've combined the years of research into a performance continuum where about 30% of people are high performers; 60% are solid performers; and 10% are low performers.

High performers are people we have the utmost confidence in. Why? They come to work ready for the day and show up on time. They have positive attitudes. They solve problems. We tend to relax when they are at work or leading an effort because we know that things are going to get accomplished. High performers are good role models and good influencers of others on the team. We're quick to call on high performers to do the most important work and take

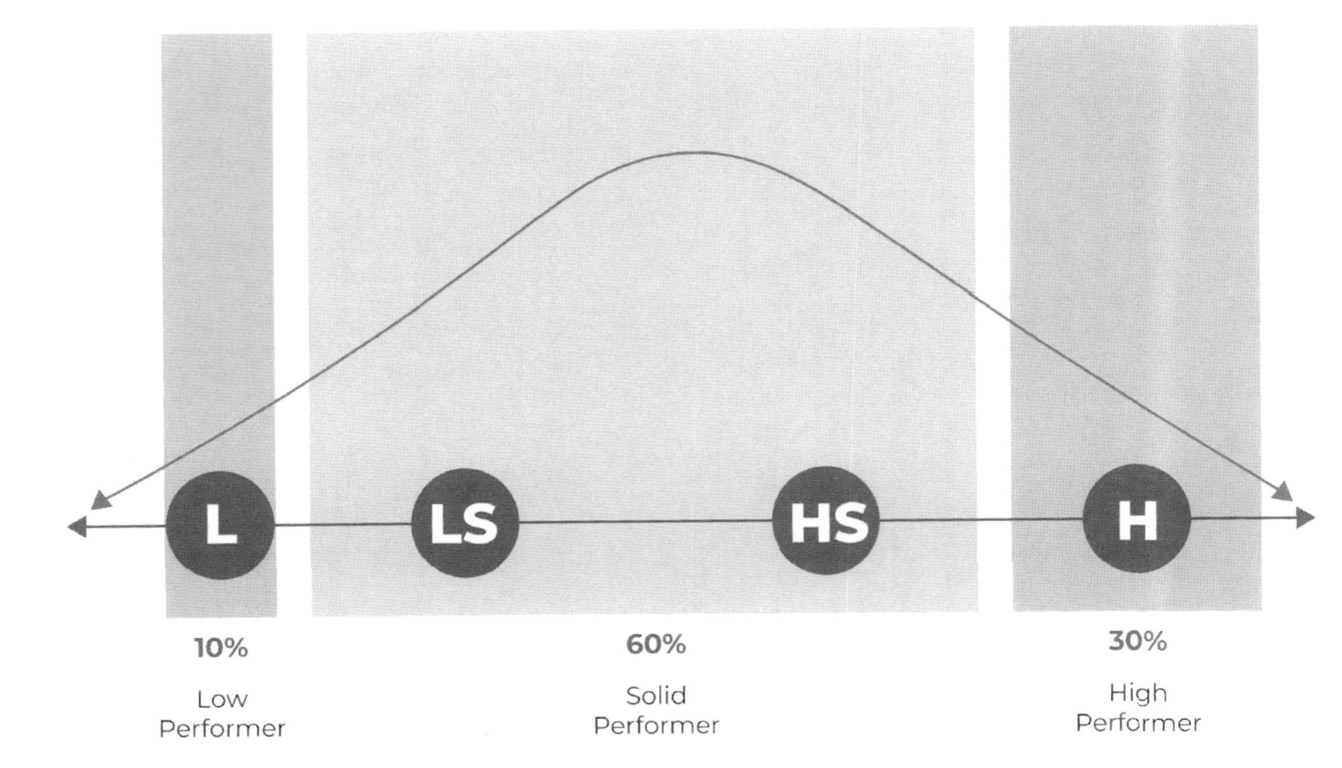


*Figure 8. Organizational Performance Curve*

on leadership roles. If there is a problem, they bring possible solutions.

Solid performers are good participants and committed to doing their best work. They want to do a good job and need good coaching from time to time. Solid performers are progressing in the right direction and are dependable to get good work done.

Most people are solid performers; they are vital to the success of our organization. There are high solid and low solid performers. High solid performers align their behaviors to high performing ones and continue down the path toward high performance with focused coaching. Low solid performers can travel toward the path of high performers or slip back to align their behaviors to low performers. They tend to be on the fence about being all in and following the organizational direction. Leaders make a difference on whether the low solid performer continues in a positive direction.

Low performers do not meet performance expectations. They tend to have bad attitudes; they point out problems without offering solutions and do it in a negative way. They manage down leadership. They are masters of we/they messages and are the first to blame their leaders. Someone else is always the problem. Low performers show little interest in improving their own performance and helping the organization achieve positive results. They may exhibit passive-aggressive behaviors.

A much tougher case is someone who really has the right attitude. This low performer is nice and helpful but doesn't have the skills to do the job right. Even so, this individual brings down the performance of the team.

Leaders can be low performers, too. You may have encountered a leader whose exhibited some of these negative behaviors or did not have the skill to lead the organization to achieve positive results. Low performing employees cannot be tolerated for long periods of time; low performing leaders have a shorter time span for turning around their performance before having to transition out of their positions. It's the leaders' responsibility to manage human performance. If a leader is a low performer that job becomes an impossible one to complete.

With the knowledge of the performance curve, leaders have every opportunity to develop about 90% of the workforce and give the other 10% an opportunity to be a contributor to the organization. If low performers fail to change, leaders must make the difficult decision to remove them from the organization. Let's look at what occurs if leaders fail to assume this responsibility.

## Keep from Hitting the Wall

As leaders advance their skills and apply the actions and tactics outlined in the Nine Principles Framework, we begin to see the performance curve come alive. Leaders see that high performers on their teams are excited to go to the next level. Solid performers remain apprehensive yet eager to make the necessary improvements. Low performers remain resistant to making the changes needed to improve. As we continue the improvement journey, our high and solid performers gain a better understanding of what the improvement journey looks and feels like.

Skilled leaders move high and solid performers to a higher level of performance. They also have the skills to move the low performers up or out of the organization within a specific timeframe. Leaders continue to hardwire key leadership behaviors to improve and stretch their teams to achieve excellence. It's not about the end game; it's about a continuous improvement process to get better and better at clearly defined goals and measures.

What occurs if leaders fail to appropriately address high, solid, and low performers? We begin to see a gap in high/solid performers and the low performers. The high/solid performers are gaining the skill set needed to move the organization forward. The low performers resist even more. The gap between the high/solid performers and the low performers is uncomfortable. This is a critical point for leadership. Leaders must have the skills to manage the discomfort. If nothing is done to address low performers, the gap becomes intolerable. The organization hits the wall, meaning the results and the improvement work slides backwards (Figure 9).

Let's take a closer look at why we hit the wall. When leaders fail to address low performers, we lose momentum with high and solid performers. Up until that point, we've continued to see progress to get over the wall with high and solid performers. The low performers negatively tug on the improvements that influence positive organizational results. There's also evidence that low performers refuse to align their behaviors to organizational values. The high and solid performers get frustrated that leaders are not holding low performers accountable.

Here's what occurs when low performance is not addressed.

- High performers don't want to be part of an organization that doesn't commit to improving and achieving positive results. If they cannot exit for some reason, they will fulfil this desire to learn and

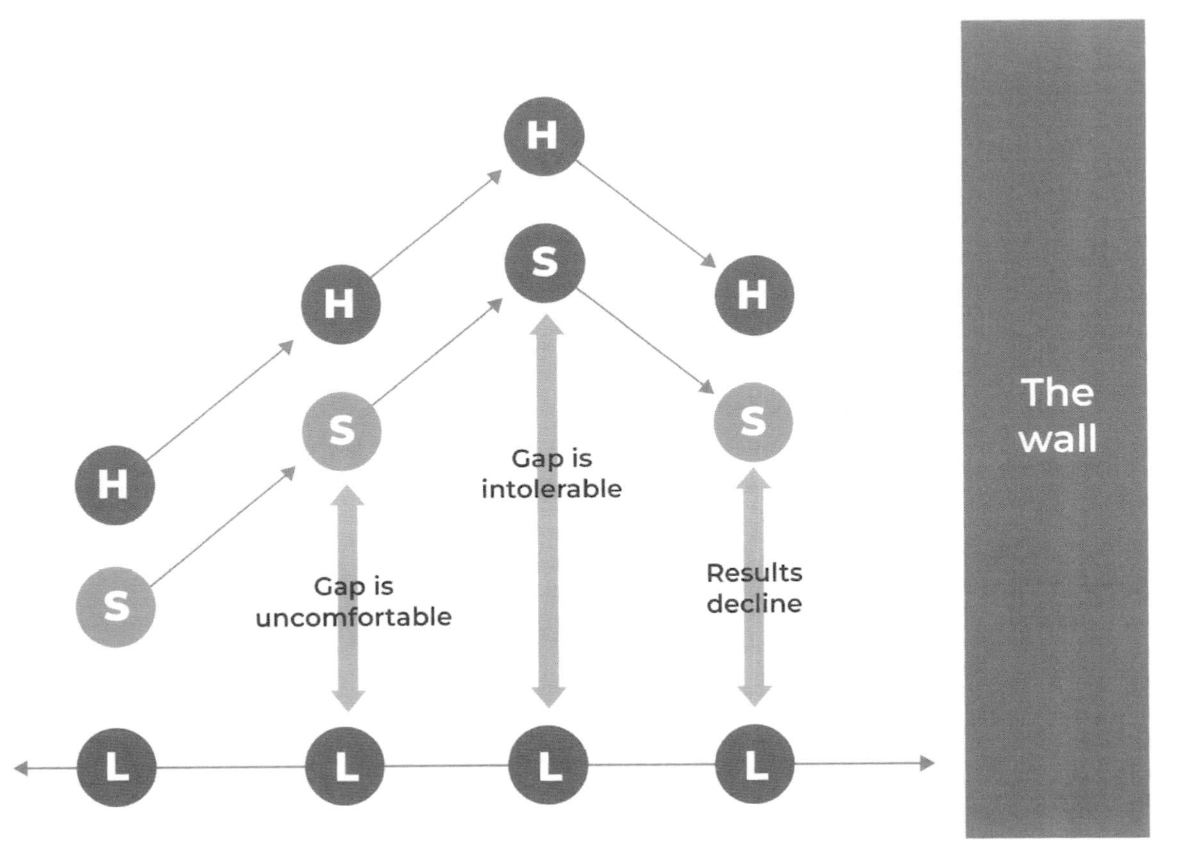


*Figure 9. Hitting the Wall*

grow by placing their energies elsewhere. They may still seem like a high performer, but they slow down and pace themselves.

- Solid performers simply slow down. They are watching what the high performers do. When they see their behavior shift, they also make shifts in their behaviors.
- The low performers continue as usual knowing they will outlast this "initiative" like they've done most of their professional lives.

Once an organization hits the wall, leaders begin to look for new approaches to the same old problems, thinking the efforts must have been misguided. We move to the next great initiative we've read or heard about, only to be disappointed down the road.

Developing leaders to support high and solid performers and address low performers is essential to achieving organizational excellence. In excellent organizations we have

- system-wide high performing results.
- the right leaders in the right place.
- a clear understanding of the keys to success by everyone in the organization.
- disciplined people and processes.
- proactive leadership.

High performing leaders build momentum to push the organization up and over the wall. A culture of excellence and improvement becomes hardwired. To get here leaders need to be trained in essential leadership skills that hardwire excellence across the board.

Developing leaders to develop people positively shifts the results up moving the performance curve to the right.

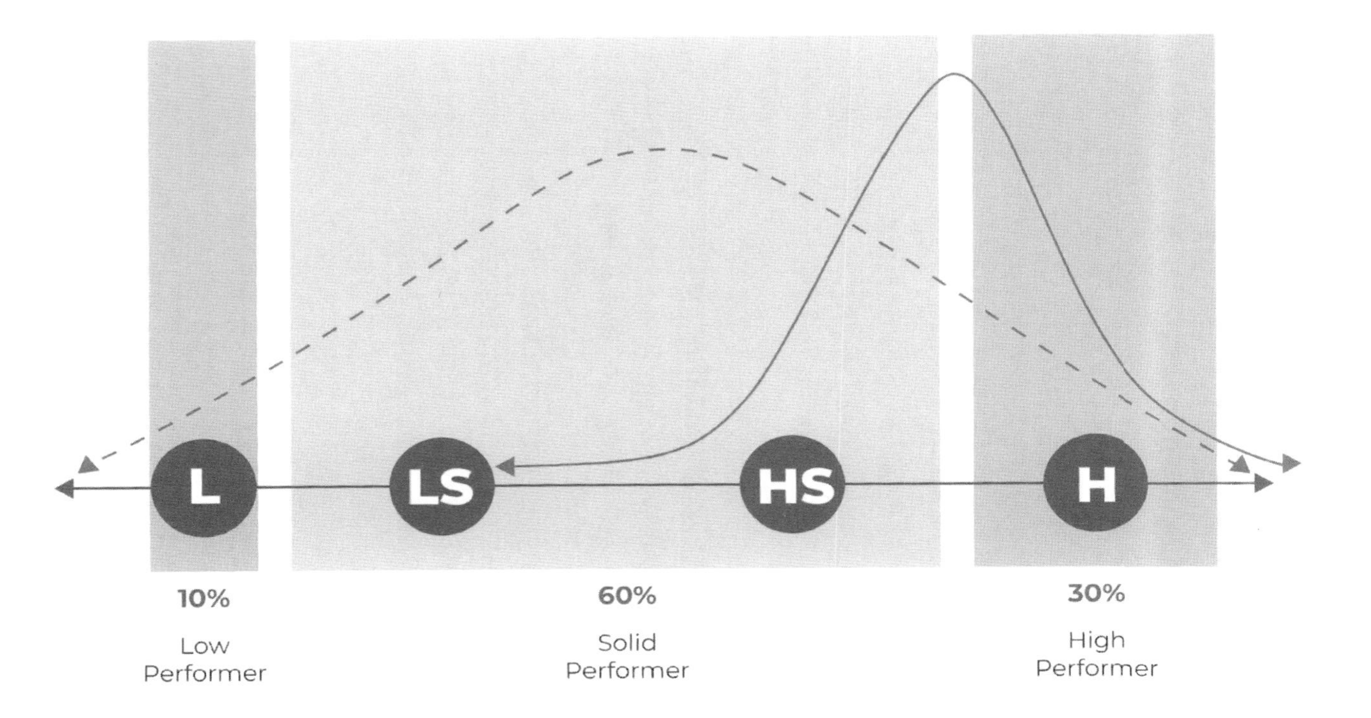


*Figure 10. Moving the Performance Curve Right and Tight*

Also, the curve becomes tighter. Individual performance is improving across the board and there is less variance in performance levels (Figure 10).

The best organizations develop their leaders to develop people to close the spread of performance levels. Excellent organizational leaders do important work by helping their organizations get over the wall and accelerate results.

## Coaching People to Be at Their Best

One of the major evolving roles of a leader is being a good coach. When I started teaching, I also coached tennis. I was a good coach and an average mathematics teacher. One day, as I walked out to the tennis courts from my day of teaching, I reflected on what a bad day I had with my classes. Being on the tennis courts with my team couldn't come soon enough. It dawned on me how unfair my thinking and actions were to my math students. What if I taught my classes like I coached tennis? My students would know what the goal was for the day, what they needed to do to achieve the goal, how that goal fit into a bigger picture, what they needed to practice to get better, how feedback could help them improve, and how to recognize their accomplishments which keeps them motivated to learn more.

From that moment on, I became a better teacher by transferring good coaching skills to my math students. I carried that with me into my leadership positions over the past three decades. Being a good coach is foundational to being a good leader. Coaching others is a job for all leaders.

We find it helpful to use a coaching conversation guide aligned to varying performance levels. We don't coach everyone the same way. We meet them where they are to help them improve. As leaders, we can't do the improvement work for them. Rather, we create opportunities for people to grow, develop, and advance their skills.

As we work with leaders, we use the following conversational guides to coach. When we coach **high performers,** we start with letting the person know where the organization is going and how their contributions matter. We specifically thank them for the ways they contribute to their team and the organization, we ask what we can do to help them, and we end with thanking them for being part of our team. High performers want to know where the organization is going, how they are helping achieve results, and what more they can do. They know where they need more help and need to be coached.

I have the pleasure of being the supervisor of a strong senior leader on our team, Dr. Melissa Matarazzo. Melissa started as one of our first coaches and grew to be the leader of our coaching team. She was recently promoted at Studer Education to assume advanced leadership roles in partnership with me. In our one-on-one coaching conversations, I enjoy spending time with Melissa talking about where we are going, what strategies will get us there, and what key results are important to focus on. Melissa always asks questions to learn and advance her knowledge and skills. I also have confidence in Melissa providing advice and direction. My goal is to support Melissa to contribute her expertise to our team. And Melissa is always asking how she can get better. That's what high performers do.

When coaching **solid performers**, we also want to recognize and appreciate their contributions. We may need to provide some specific examples of how their work helped achieve results. We recognize them for living the values in a positive way. We ask probing questions about areas not working as well. We get them to help us define the performance problem or barrier in order to derive a solution. As we begin the excellence journey, most of our people are solid performers, ranging from low solid to high solid performers.

With a little coaching, **high solid performers** can help us solve problems or contribute a new idea. We start with identifying a problem and asking probing questions about the problem. We then ask high solid performers if they have questions that we could answer together to continue to understand the problem at hand. The goal is not to jump to solutions but to dive into a deep conversation identifying the problem at hand. I've found that high solid performers are good at having deeper conversations and thinking critically as we guide and coach them through the conversation. On the other hand, individuals who jump to solutions right away may be good, solid performers living closer to the middle of the curve. They need more direction during our coaching sessions.

**Low solid performers** need structure and direction from leaders. They may not see that certain areas of their performance need to be improved. We still provide positive recognition for the things they are doing well to reduce their anxieties and capitalize on the good before we provide improvement feedback. It's important for us to remember the 3 to 1 principle – 3 positive comments to 1 constructive comment ends in a positive action.

Here's what I've discovered. Low solid performers tend to have difficulty listening. They seldom probe for deeper understanding. Therefore, as leaders, we need to structure our conversations with low performers. The low solid performers may be anxious, fear failing, and are trying to prove themselves. We spend more time preparing for low solid performer conversations. It takes pre-work to structure the conversation. The conversations include specific intentions toward achieving an outcome and good follow-up.

Let's say we have a low solid performer who does not work as well as needed with the team and fails to recognize this is occurring. Our goal is to provide the low solid performer with an expected outcome and specific behaviors to work on. We first point out some positive aspects of their work. Then we describe the problem at hand and give specific examples of what the low solid performer is doing that interferes with being a good team member. We ask low solid performers to tell us what they heard. We provide specific behaviors for the individual to focus on with a follow-up approach to continue coaching. For the low solid performers to move up the curve, we must see evidence of changed behavior. Otherwise, they shift toward the low performer end of the curve.

Here's the great news. Leaders can coach about 90% of their team members in positive and productive ways. I've found that most people like to receive feedback and talk about what they can do to improve. The way we approach coaching conversations influences the way people improve.

In 2010, the first day I started at Studer Group, I met with the CEO, Quint Studer. I asked him what he wanted me to do first. He reached over on his desk, retrieved a piece of paper and pen and wrote this note – *"Janet Pilcher can do whatever Janet Pilcher believes is the best thing to do."* He signed it, *"Quint Studer."* In some ways I was terrified of this responsibility. On the other hand, I was excited and eager. I started building the strategic direction of Studer Education.

Quint also knew I needed coaching. He planned a leadership development session with a special education service provider in Northern Chicago where he facilitated the session. He asked me to take notes for us to talk about. We had another leader session planned right outside of St. Paul, Minnesota. When we finished in Chicago, he suggested that we drive instead of fly. This gave us hours in the car together. He took me through his former hometown in Janesville, Wisconsin. We stopped and had dinner with his daughter and grandchildren at Mac's Pizza Shack. We drove north through the Wisconsin Dells. He told me stories about him and his family camping in the Dells. As we were driving, he pulled off at an exit in the Dells and said he was taking me to see the neatest McDonald's in the country. We continued our travels to St. Paul where I again watched him work his magic with leaders and then coach me on lessons he had learned over the years. As my coach, what did Quint do? He spent valuable time with me, introduced me to him in more meaningful ways, modeled how to develop leaders, and coached me through conversations. I was not skilled at my new job, which felt terrifying considering I left a position as an experienced leader. He helped me work through my discomfort and take on new challenges that would lead to some failures and successes. Just as Quint coached me, a good coach cares about developing people to be at their best.

## Critical Conversations

One of the most popular questions we get is, what do I do with low performers? Low performers tend to coast along in the organization, doing as little work as they can to get by, collecting their paychecks, and infecting others with their negative attitudes. High performers usually try to dodge low performers, and solid performers walk on eggshells working alongside them. Our employees deserve to be protected from low performers' negativity or poor skills. Leaders are the individuals in an organization who can make this occur.

Remember, low performers are masters at blaming and diverting problems. During the critical conversation, they may blame others for their low performance, blame you for not giving them enough training or resources, and unload personal problems to play on your sympathies attempting to divert the conversation away from their performance.

As leaders, we may rationalize the situation to keep from having the conversation. We may say, *"A warm body is better than not having someone"* or *"At least we know what we are dealing with. If we hire someone else, we may have a whole new set of problems."* I've had leaders ask me this question, *"What if someone is a high performing employee, but no one wants to be on their team or work with them."* I answer, *"That's a low performer."* People who fail to live the values have a negative effect on others. That connects us back to Principle 1 Commit to Excellence. As difficult as it is, we must address low performing behaviors. Our teams depend on us.

In my 30 years in leadership, engaging in critical conversations with low performers remains the most difficult part of the job. To almost every detail, I still remember the low performing conversations I've had over the years, including those when I had to let someone go. The experience sits at the top of my heart and mind. I also know that in each circumstance, it was the right decision. It's the loneliest place and the part of the job where we have the least experience. The critical conversation structure helps leaders follow an approach that builds confidence and guidance.

Once people demonstrate they are unwilling to improve, it's time to engage in a critical conversation with them. We shift from coaching to holding them accountable. If an individual is causing harm in any way toward others or creating an extremely toxic work environment, we immediately work with our human resources colleagues to address the toxic behaviors and ensure the safety of others.

Critical conversations occur with people who have consistently exhibited behaviors that go against organizational values or demonstrate subpar performance. We may find that we've not done a great job with documenting low performers' negative behaviors. That doesn't mean we can't move forward. Quite the opposite, it's now time. Our high and solid performers deserve a better work environment. They shouldn't have to work with low performers.

The first step is to build alignment with your supervisor and Human Resources. Lay everything out and gain guidance on how to proceed with the process and conversation. Our human resources colleagues want to do the right thing; they will be a good resource regardless of where you start the process of addressing low performers.

We've successfully guided leaders on following what we've called over the years, the DESK approach. Here's an important tip. Don't start the conversation off on a positive note. Start right with the issue at hand.

First, start with the **D or Describe** the specific issue you are addressing. Be very clear about the problem. We then move to the **E or Evaluate** exactly where the person is not meeting expectations, how that makes people feel, and how their behavior impacts the results. Now we move to **S, which means show** the low performer what needs to be done to improve. We follow with **K**, which stands for the low performer **knowing the consequences**. We spell out the consequences for the behavior as well as the consequences if the behavior continues.

The low performer may think that once they're out the door, life will return to normal. So, it's vital that we talk about

**follow-up**; how often we're going to meet with them, what the meetings will look like, and what we expect them to do between now and then. Here's the point. Make sure the low performer knows that our expectations are clear, and we are committed to ensuring their performance improves. The low performer's job is to sustain good performance over time to move from a low to solid performer.

We find that one-third of the low performers will self-select out. Once they realize they can no longer do what they've been doing, they may leave. Another third will adjust their behavior. The remaining third will have to be directed to leave.

When we have low performers in our organizations, they can take up to 80% of our time. Our goal is to flip that to spend at least 80% of the time on high and solid performers. Remember, only about 1 in 10 people may be low performers at the onset. Most people want to be developed to improve their skills so that they can contribute to the organization.

## Executive Leaders Must Be High Performers

In this chapter, we've reviewed the typical spread of human performance across the organization while reinforcing that our role as leaders is to support and develop people to move the performance curve right and tight. That is, we want to gain consistent performance at the top end of the curve with most people performing at high levels. Simply put, high performing people produce high performing organizational results. That's why developing leaders to develop people is one of our nine principles.

Moving the performance curve right and tight (higher results by people consistently performing at the highest levels) depends on executive leaders being high performers or what Jim Collins calls Level 5 Leaders. He identified 5 characteristics of Level 5 leaders from his intensive study of high performing organizations. Level 5 leaders have a

- personal sense of humility.
- deep personal understanding of one's strengths and weaknesses.
- laser-like focus on the organization's purpose.
- passionate commitment to continuous learning.
- relentless determination to do what is right, not what is easy.

We are fortunate to work with executive leaders who commit to being high performers. Here's an example of what a high performing executive looks like. Dr. Matt Hillmann is the superintendent of Northfield Public Schools, Minnesota. Northfield Public Schools is a southeastern Minnesota school district serving families in Northfield and surrounding areas. I had the pleasure of meeting Dr. Hillmann several years ago at one of our conferences. His presentation made a lasting impression on me. I've followed his progress over the years. As I am writing this book, Dr. Hillmann has been recognized as one of four finalists for the 2023 American Association of School Administrator's National Superintendent of the Year award. He practices all nine principles in *Hardwiring Excellence in Education*. Connected to this chapter's principle, he and his team have taken the performance curve to the next level by specifically applying it to Northfield Public Schools. He led the district to develop a tool that includes descriptors of performance for the levels along the performance curve. These performance descriptors are transparent to all employees in the district. He gathered input throughout the district to create the final product that clearly defines performance expectations.

Let's review some additional examples of how Dr. Hillmann exhibits Level 5 leadership. Dr. Hillmann is focused on ensuring that every student is successful. He uses data to inform his team on how well they are doing. Here's one example. Dr. Hillmann and his team doubled down on a long-standing problem in the district. Hispanic students were graduating at a rate of 36%. He brought his community together to solve this problem to improve the graduation rate. Along with other actions, the district continued a focused effort called The Torch Program. These actions quickly moved the graduation rate for these students to 97%. In an *Accelerate Your Performance* podcast episode, I asked Dr. Hillmann how they achieved such significant results. He said, *"First, it's recognizing that we are fellow human beings. Fellow human beings want to have a relationship. Parents and families want to be included and know that their children are cared for and tended to when they're at school. The first part is showing up. I think we can make a lot of excuses or find different ways to not show up. Showing up means being vulnerable and open to acknowledging that we're learning about a culture. We're learning how to interact. We're learning the best way to serve families from different immigrant backgrounds."*

Dr. Hillmann led his team to take specific actions to improve the graduation results. Here's an example of how his team focused on strengthening their communication approaches with Hispanic families.

- Anything sent from the Superintendent's office isn't sent until it's been translated (first starting with a Google translation and then adjusted where needed by an actual person).
- Anytime the district sends an email to Spanish speaking families, they also get a voice message from a Spanish translator (this allows them to serve families despite literacy).

- They have a two-way texting program – the texts are interpreted before transmission.
- They created a system that supports families connecting with the schools at a time that's convenient for them.

Strengthening communication approaches as well as other actions made a difference in the lives of students and their families. Dr. Hillmann received the 2022 Human Rights Award in recognition of his work to improve support for immigrant families and the dedication he demonstrated to listen to the Hispanic Community in Northfield. The most powerful aspect of this award is that he was nominated by the Hispanic parents and families he and his team served.

It's easy to see that Dr. Hillmann is open to input and feedback. Here are several more ways he demonstrates being a high performer. He is completely transparent with his leaders when making decisions, especially tough ones. He uses processes that give each leader a chance to provide input and speak freely. He uses two tools described in this book, "Plus/Delta" and the "5 Whys." One of his favorite process tools is "Fist of Five." This tool helps leaders view the various commitment levels of agreement with a decision. We are accustomed to a "yes" or "no" vote. The "Fist of Five" asks people to vote by raising hands and showing the number of fingers raised that indicates their level of agreement with the decision.

- A fist means "no."
- 1 finger means "I'll just barely go along."
- 2 fingers means "I don't like this, but I'll go along."
- 3 fingers means, "I'm in the middle somewhere. Like some of it, but not all."
- 4 fingers means, "This is fine."

- 5 fingers means, "I like this a lot, I think it's the best possible decision."

Once leaders complete the decision-making process, they have a frank discussion about their votes while working toward solutions they will all support.

The examples show how Dr. Hillmann has a laser-like focus on the organization's purpose and a relentless determination to do what is right, not what is easy. He also has humility, wants input on his strengths and where he can improve, and is a continuous learner. Dr. KK Owen serves as the leader coach for Northfield Public Schools. He proactively asks KK to provide personal feedback on his strengths as a leader and where he can improve. When I was debriefing with KK, she told me a story about Dr. Hillmann. KK was onsite with one of our newly hired leader coaches in Northfield. Dr. Hillmann asked KK to observe a leadership session where *big* issues were being addressed that would lead to *big* decisions being made. The new coach asked Dr. Hillmann if she could sit in the debrief session with KK and him as KK provided feedback on the leadership session. He said, "yes, of course," and during the debrief session he even welcomed feedback from new coach he had just met that morning.

Humility is to admit that you don't always know the answers or have the best solutions, and that you need help to succeed. The two decades of research by Dr. Brené Brown introduces vulnerability as a relevant and necessary characteristic of high performing executives and leaders. Vulnerability is the courage to put yourself out there and have the courage to take risks. Dr. Hillmann provides a great example of these two characteristics of high performing leadership.

I asked KK - what is most powerful about Dr. Hillmann's leadership? She said, *"It is his openness to receive feedback, describe what he learns from the feedback, and change his behaviors to improve."* She's witnessed that first-hand with their one-on-one conversations and her observations with his leaders, employees, parents, and the broader community. He does so because he is laser focused on the organization's purpose – to provide an environment where each student is successful.

We are grateful for executive leaders like Dr. Hillmann. They make us better leader coaches and people. Organizations can't be excellent without high performing leaders; leaders can't be excellent without high performing executives; and executives can't be excellent without a high performing executive leader. It takes high performing leaders to develop high performing people. That's the way we move the performance curve right and tight.

## Chapter 4 Summary

When we consistently apply key leadership skills, make the Standards of Excellence a core part of the hiring process, re-recruit high performers, develop solid performers, and hold low performers accountable, we reduce the performance issues across the board. We contribute to creating a workplace environment that reinvigorates our teams to do meaningful work. That's the type of place more people want to work. That type of workplace is possible when we have high performing executive leaders who commit to and act on developing leaders to develop people.

Leaders have an awesome responsibility when it comes to developing and coaching people. That's why leadership development is essential. To be an excellent organization we must hire and retain excellent people. That just doesn't occur naturally. Leaders need good training in a consistent way that specifically aligns to their daily responsibilities. Good training includes learning evidence-based tactics, practicing them, applying the tactics in the field, and reflecting on what worked and didn't work. Good training, then, is not isolated from daily work. We develop leaders and other employees on the most pressing needs to close performance gaps that get in the way of achieving positive results. Now let's focus on tried- and true- tactics that are an important part of leadership development and connected to building inspiring workplace environments. Principle 5 Focus on Employee Engagement describes tools and tactics to do just that.

# 5

# FOCUS ON EMPLOYEE ENGAGEMENT

*Attend to aspirations and desires in the workplace.*

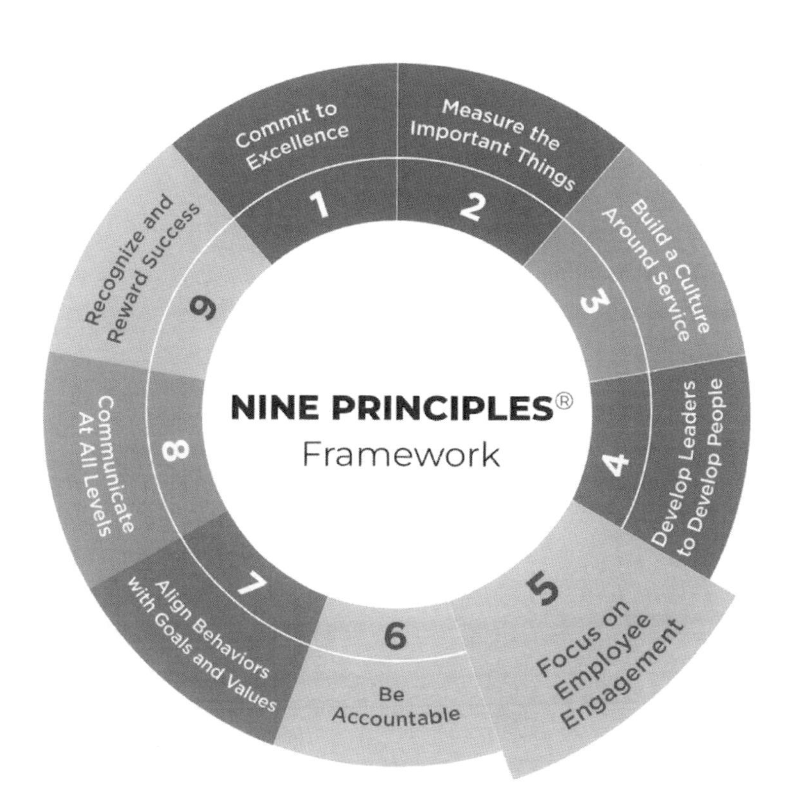

Most employees want to do purposeful work. They want to know what they do is worthwhile and makes a difference. A prerequisite for these three conditions occurring is the first rung of the organizational flywheel – inspiring workplaces.

Instructional leaders are trained to focus on instructional and academic leadership. Operational leaders may attend training sessions to achieve industry certifications. In education, we've spent little if any time training leaders on the best ways to create a workplace environment that engages employees and delivers excellent service. These skills include connecting people to goals, engaging them in meaningful conversations to achieve the goals, providing good feedback to help them improve their performance, creating ways for them to work together to solve problems, and recognizing and appreciating what they do.

A workplace with engaged employees feels good. It's a place where employees tend to go the extra mile. They remain highly committed to serving students and their families and enjoy working with their colleagues. A study by the American Psychological Association found 93% of employees who reported feeling valued said that they are motivated to do their best at work and 88% reported feeling engaged. When people feel valued, they are

- more trusting in each other.
- likely to help each other out.
- more confident in themselves.
- happier at work and in life.
- more resilient with less stress.

Good leaders see their role in building inspiring workplace environments. This chapter focuses on tactics that help leaders do just that. Principle 5 is Focus on Employee Engagement. This chapter connects employee engagement with the educational core values, summarizes the employee engagement survey and roll out process, describes leader rounding, and presents ways to coach people in the moment.

## Connecting Employee Engagement to Values

How do we build inspiring workplace environments that engage employees? Let's go back to the three educational core values – purpose, worthwhile work, and making a difference.

1. *Employees want to believe their organization has the right purpose, and they want to know how what they do connects to that purpose.* Senior leaders set the vision and direction of the organization. As we work through the various ranks, it's more likely for fewer and fewer people to know where the organization is going. Consequently, people come to work and do their jobs with little understanding about the significance of what they do. Have you heard people say, *"The senior level leaders have no idea what I do. They need to come to where I work to see what I do."* Do people want senior leaders to hang out with them while they do their work? Probably not. They simply

want to believe senior leaders know and care about what they do. Employees want to know what they do contributes to the organization and to be recognized by leaders.

2. *Employees want to know their work is worthwhile.* They want to know what they do is important to the organization. Leaders help their teams see how their work contributes to the overall results. Teachers see how what they do helps students succeed. Bus drivers see how they help students get to school safely. Cafeteria workers see that providing a healthy meal to students makes a difference in students being able to learn. Educational service departments see how they help people in the organization do their jobs better. We may assume that employees know these things. This wrong assumption disheartens people. Leaders are not responsible for employees being motivated. They are responsible for showing employees how their contributions matter to overall organizational health.
3. *Employees want to make a difference.* Those of us who choose the education profession are passionate about our work. Seeing positive results fuels our passion. When we work on something and see improvements, we want to work harder to continue to improve. What keeps us motivated? Reviewing how we are doing, having conversations with each other about the bright spots, and seeing the results we've accomplished. Employees also like to be part of finding solutions to problems. Most answers can be found with people in our organizations. That's why we apply processes that engage employees in conversations about what's working and what's not. It's even better when we use data to facilitate improvement conversations among teams.

Here's one of my proudest stories of our team applying actions to live the educational core values – purpose, worthwhile work, and making a difference. As I made a career change from the university to Studer Group, Quint Studer gave me an open door to build a plan to start Studer Education. I took the first step to do so. During my tenure as dean of a college, I created an alternative teacher certification program, TeacherReady. I reconnected with the university to leverage a partnership to transition the alternative certification program to Studer Education. We moved forward with a good partnership which gave me an opportunity to nurture and grow the program I was passionate about.

TeacherReady is a state approved, nationally accredited online program that's been in existence for two decades. We've certified over 4000 teachers around the world. We've managed to grow the program and attain high marks on teachers entering the field and remaining in the profession. Our TeacherReady team, led by Dr. Sarah Miller, remains highly engaged in applying a continuous improvement process to update the program and keep it relevant. Their level of engagement to apply a continuous improvement process to achieve meaningful goals reinforces their value and contribution to the program and each other.

Reviewing student input and quality measures, the TeacherReady team suggested making meaningful changes over the years that are cutting edge in the way college programs are offered. Here are a few of the modifications made. Our team

- continuously updates a standard curriculum using feedback on each of the program lessons.
- trains instructors to provide timely, continuous, and meaningful narrative feedback to students rather than assigning a grade.

- assigns advisors that stay with students throughout the program and engages in meaningful relationships with the instructors and the students' mentors.
- enrolls students every day, seven days a week.
- hires instructors throughout the country who have expertise in the content areas to provide highly focused, quality feedback to students.
- places students in classrooms with mentor teachers wherever they live in the world.
- implements a course to assist students with preparing for the state certification tests.

These actions represent ways we've shifted over the years to offer the program to meet students where they are and with what they need. The TeacherReady team reviews student data every week to ensure that students have a great experience. The team engages in conversations about the data that gives them confidence to make improvement decisions that are in the best interest of the students. Consequently, our higher education model has disrupted the traditional way of doing business. We've done so while maintaining quality outcomes.

Creating an environment where people have purpose, do worthwhile work, and make a difference is the challenge and the work for leaders to do. Taking on that challenge with the TeacherReady team early on in Studer Education made me a better leader. I learned that when employees know how what they do makes a difference in the lives of others, they become engaged in their work. The team's work offers students an opportunity to achieve their dream of becoming a teacher.

## Employee Engagement Survey and Roll Out Process

Let's face it. People are complex. Building inspiring workplaces is an art and an inexact science. I'm a fan of gaining input from employees. So, that's where we start. Perception data doesn't tell us exactly where problems exist, nor does it always represent the whole picture. That's why it's important to receive input in various ways to understand how employees feel about their work. We can openly gather information or let negativity circulate and escalate at the water cooler. On the upside, input can also be positive.

We recommend conducting an employee survey along with a roll out process. A survey alone reduces the value of the tool. Unfortunately, administering an employee engagement survey without doing something with the results is typical. We ask our employees to complete the survey. The leaders get the results. In our experience, most of the time leaders don't share the results with employees. Even more, they don't talk about the results nor take action to improve. When employees take time to complete a survey, we owe it to them to share and use the results to improve. We value our employees by using the data to engage in meaningful conversations with them.

We work with organizations to apply a Studer Employee Survey and Roll Out Process. Once the survey is complete, we analyze and report the results to organizations. We train leaders on how to explain the results to their teams and create a consistent and timely roll out process. Leaders throughout the organization are responsible for rolling out the results following a defined and consistent process.

Here's the step-by-step process we use with organizations.

1. *We administer the survey, analyze the results, and share the results reports.* The administration process includes crafting key words in a message from the executive leader describing why the survey is important and how the employees' input will help the organization create a positive workplace culture. The message includes how the results will be shared and used to create improvement action plans. The goal is to get high participation rates. Because our organizational leaders apply a survey roll out process along with administering the employee surveys, most of our partner organizations have a 70% or higher response rate on the survey. An organizational results report and individual leader reports serve as key tools for leaders to use to roll out the results. Importantly, we ensure that we apply a survey process that keeps individual employee responses confidential.

2. *We train leaders on how to interpret the results and share the results with their teams.* This includes the executive leader presenting the organizational results and then individual leaders sharing their results with their teams.
3. *We train senior leaders on the steps of the roll out process prior to launching the leader input sessions.* We start with senior leaders engaging in conversations about the organizational results by sharing areas working well and those needing improvements.
4. *The senior leaders communicate to employees the expectations for leaders rolling out the survey results and creating improvement actions.* The leader also provides a timeline for when the roll out process will occur.

5. *Each leader rolls out the results following a consistent process.* Leaders focus on both the positive and challenging areas. They continue to engage employees in conversations about what actions can be taken to improve the workplace environment.
6. *The collective dialogue results in 1 to 3 improvement actions.* Teams become more engaged when they are part of the solution. We want to focus more effort on fewer things to get improved results. We've found that when we focus on one area, we tend to improve in other areas. We may focus on one survey question where we need to improve, apply a few actions, and then assess the progress every 45 to 75 days.
7. *The improvement action plans are shared with the senior team.* This team analyzes the areas for improvement, looks for patterns in the improvement actions, and uses the information to determine core actions worth focusing on across the organization.
8. *Senior leaders apply a follow-up process to check in on how well the improvements are working throughout the organization.* Senior leaders ask leaders what they've learned as their teams implemented the improvement actions. Senior leaders may elect to add this process to their leadership team agendas each month or engage in conversations during monthly one-on-one meetings with leaders.
9. *The Studer Employee Survey is administered at least once a year to determine the progress made.* We've designed our survey to align with employee engagement research and to be short, simple, and focused. It's important to note, if organizations

use other employee engagement surveys, we train leaders on how to apply the survey roll out process using the data leaders have at hand.

I admit, I still get anxious when I review the results of the Employee Engagement survey. Let's face it. Receiving feedback from others is an emotional experience. Positive feedback feels good. Negative feedback even when provided in a constructive way feels bad.

It's difficult to hear messages that challenge our thinking and doing. When I hear negative information, my instinct is to say things like *"only the angry people complete surveys," "the sample size is small,"* and *"something's wrong with the survey."* I also want to rationalize why something didn't work, couldn't work, or would never work. I start to blame other people. I think, *"If other departments would do their job, the problems in our area wouldn't occur and people would be happier."* Our natural tendency when receiving negative feedback is to deny, rationalize, and blame. Once I work through these initial emotions, I turn my attention to rolling out the results to determine how we can improve.

Let's focus on how we review the data. Leaders review the overall mean of the survey and means by items. We also ask leaders to review a top box percentage. The overall mean provides an average of the responses. The top box shows how many people scored each item at the highest level on the scale. We recommend that leaders think about how we move 3s to 4s and 4s to 5s on a 5-point scale. Why? Because when we are serious about improving, it's easier to improve the perceptions of people who feel good about the organization than it is to shift those who are assessing the workplace environment at the lowest level. We want people who feel good about the workplace to shift to feeling great.

When viewing narrative feedback, we recommend that leaders place the feedback into four categories – positive, neutral, negative, and not constructive. Here's what I mean by the last category. Some comments are not useful to inform improvements, such as "everything is good," "love working here," "everything is bad," "the culture is terrible," "everyone's unhappy," and so on. Here's an example of how a certain type of comment falls into the four categories. The first three categories provide useful information.

- Positive: People are recognized in timely and specific ways.
- Neutral: There's been an effort to recognize people in timely and specific ways. This is positive but not followed by all leaders.
- Negative: We've heard that recognition is important, but it's not done often. When it is, it doesn't seem genuine. We hear things like "everyone's doing a good job." And we know not everyone is.
- Not constructive: Working here is a joke. No one feels appreciated.

Our tendency is to quickly go to the negative and non- constructive feedback. Remember, non-constructive, negative statements represent low performing behaviors. It's impossible to build improvement actions from these comments. Therefore, push them aside and focus on the positive, neutral, and negative constructive comments. And start with the positive.

Employees have both positive and negative feelings about certain aspects of the workplace environment. We can train people in how to provide positive and negative feedback using helpful messages. We can't assume that employees know how to do this well or understand what the expectations are when providing feedback to others. We help employees see that using the survey to complain by writing general messages doesn't help improve the workplace environment. Here are the learning outcomes for an employee training session.

- Describe the goal for providing comments on an employee engagement survey.
- Describe why it is important for employees to provide timely and specific feedback to help improve the workplace environment.
- Review and analyze a general, non-constructive statement.
- Review and analyze a constructive statement.
- Describe the differences between the two statements and how the constructive statement provides more meaningful feedback.
- Re-write a non-constructive statement to make it a constructive statement.

As mentioned, it's important to do something about the results. In the survey roll out process, we train leaders to start with the positives. Why? There's usually a lot more positive than negative. Our solid and high performers take time to point out the positives in the most constructive ways. They also take time to give constructive feedback in areas where we can improve.

Administering, reporting, and rolling out an employee survey gives employees a way to offer feedback about their workplace environment. It helps us know what we are doing well and where we need to improve. The survey roll out process moves people's input to actionable improvements. We do more of what we are doing well and improve where we have gaps in our performance. By doing so we continuously build an inspiring workplace.

One of our partners, Child Development Center, Inc. (CDC) achieved powerful employee engagement results. Dr. Rina Irwin is the CEO of the organization and one of our Difference Maker Award recipients. CDC provides high quality learning to children from infancy through sixth grade. CDC has 14 early learning centers in northwestern Pennsylvania serving approximately 2,000 early learners. In 5 years, CDC has grown from 5 early learning centers to 14. They employ right at 400 people. CDC supports the many needs of a child with board certified pediatricians, speech therapists, mental health consultants, child well-being specialists, family engagement specialists, and degreed preschool teachers.

Over these 5 years, CDC has improved their employee engagement scores and participation rates. They've improved from a 3.98 to 4.02 mean score on a 5-point scale and currently have a 97.5% participation rate. The positive results have occurred as CDC has witnessed tremendous growth.

During the survey administration, employees receive several messages focused on how important their input is to build a positive workplace culture. Immediately after CDC receives the results, the departments send a specific message to employees. In this message the employees receive the results for the organization and their specific departments. Dr. Irwin and her team recognize that the quicker the communication occurs with results, the easier it is to keep an employee's interest in the survey process.

Dr. Irwin tells the story about her Studer Education coach Dr. Kathy Oropallo asking their leadership team why they believed it was important to pursue every employee's feedback. They responded – *"because every employee matters."* Dr. Irwin and her team have worked hard to establish an inspiring workplace. The results show the work is making a difference. CDC not only administers the employee engagement surveys, but they also apply the tactics outlined in this chapter, including leader rounding, 30- & 90-day conversations, stoplight reports, and continuous anonymous feedback on workplace environment improvement actions.

Another leader who has been highly committed to building an engaged workplace culture and seeking input using an employee survey is Dr. Kyle Marrero, President of Georgia Southern University. I've heard him say that the secret sauce to creating a great organization is having a continuous drive to improve and the perseverance to achieve excellence.

One of Dr. Marrero's key strategic priorities is to administer the survey to all Georgia Southern University employees and apply the roll out process summarized in this chapter. Most all leaders receive an individual leader report providing them with specific results from their direct reports. Dr. Marrero applies a process where his executive team collects and monitors Employee Engagement Action Plans for all leaders in their respective divisions. In addition, Dr. Marrero presents the university results at a virtual Town Hall meeting. Leaders then participate in leader training on the roll out process, they roll out the results, and they complete their action plans that outline their improvement actions during the year.

Dr. Marrero is committed to developing leaders and people in institutions he leads. The overarching theme of the Georgia Southern Strategic Plan is *People. Purpose. Action: Growing Ourselves to Grow Others!* Leaders at Georgia Southern University are expected to be open to feedback, act on it, and transform themselves to be better leaders and people. Dr. Marrero expects that and more of himself. He models the way for his leadership team. In his own words, *"Striving and achieving organizational excellence is a continuous process of growth and improvement, and you, as a leader, have to be willing to look in mirror because it might be you who is holding the organization back."* This is important advice for all of us in leadership positions.

## Leader Rounding

We focused on service rounding as a core tactic for Principle 3 Build a Culture Around Service. One of the most important tactics to improve employee engagement is leader rounding. We've heard our partner organizational leaders tell us in times of tremendous change, leader rounding helps them manage change in the most effective ways.

Leader rounding is a great tactic that helps leaders communicate openly and consistently with employees. We find out what's going well at work and what's getting in the way of employees being able to do their best work. Leader rounding is the most important tactic to help individuals engage in their work environment. That's why we put leader rounding as a fundamental leadership skill.

Before I knew what rounding was, I thought I rounded with employees. I remember when I was the dean of a college, I walked the halls. I walked down the hall and gave employees a quick wave as I passed by. I might stick my head in an office or two asking, *"How are you doing?"* Usually they'd say, *"Fine."* I would say, *"Glad to hear it."* And provide them with a "well-wish" and be on my way. I imagine they were rolling their eyes saying, *"There she goes again."*

Leader rounding is different from what I thought it was. You see, I really cared about the people who worked in our college. But I failed to make deeper connections with people that showed them I cared. Intentionally rounding with faculty and staff would have made me a better leader.

Leader rounding is intentional and focused on what employees are looking for in their leaders. They want

- to have a good relationship with their leader.
- their leader to be approachable and sincere.
- a willingness in their leader to work side by side with them.
- systems to work smoothly and resources to do their jobs.
- to be trained and developed.
- to feel appreciated and cared for as an employee and person.

An initial goal for leaders is to build relationships with people – get to know them, what they like, and what they relate to. We want to know about the people who are most important to them, and other things that define them as individuals. Leaders round to show they care about employees' well-being. Leaders want to provide an inspiring workplace environment for everyone to feel satisfied and happy at work. They want to make sure employees are challenged and supported. Remember, people want three major things at work. They want to work for an organization that keeps purpose, worthwhile work, and making a difference at the forefront. Employees want to work with leaders who model these educational core values.

Let's dig into the leader rounding tactic. Deborah McIntyre's work is essential to our success as she serves in the role of supporting our senior leadership team and me to support, grow, and sustain our organization. Her daily work includes coordinating and supporting my connection with our team and the executives of our partner organizations.

Rounding with Deborah, I make a personal connection with her. I may ask about her grandchildren or her trip to Germany to visit her nephew. Sometimes, I simply ask how she is doing in general. She is always concerned about my well-being. I take this moment to be concerned about her on a deeper and more personal level. I then ask Deborah the leader rounding questions and engage in a meaningful conversation with her. I pay ridiculous attention by listening and hearing what she has to say. I probe to understand more. I ask

1. Over the past week or so, what's going well?
2. What's getting in the way of you doing your best work?
3. Who has been especially helpful to you?
4. Is there anything I could do to be helpful to you?

I thank Deborah for always being proactive and responsive in helping me manage my time, schedule, and projects. I express my gratitude to Deborah for caring about my well-being. After the session, I transfer my notes to actionable items, determine people that need to be recognized, and jot down barriers to follow up on.

An important part of the rounding process is recording the information from the session including people who were recognized, why they were recognized, and barriers to address. We recommend that leaders use a stoplight report to tackle barriers that surface during rounding conversations. Leaders accumulate weekly rounding information on the stoplight report. Addressed items are coded green. Items in progress are coded yellow. Items that can't be addressed are coded in red with a sentence or two by the item explaining why it can't be addressed. The stoplight report is shared with leaders and employees so they can see the follow-up from the rounding sessions. Also, leaders can apply the tools and tactics in Chapter 9 to recognize and appreciate individuals noted in the rounding sessions. Over time, we've found that leader rounding is one of the most powerful tactics for building positive employee relationships and attending to employees' aspirations and desires in the workplace.

Leader rounding is versatile. One of the first questions people ask is, "Do I have to ask the rounding questions you suggest?" Of course, we have the freedom to make changes that are meaningful if the purpose behind the approach is followed. Remember,

- make a meaningful, personal connection.
- start with a positive question.
- gain understanding of potential barriers.
- include ways for people to recognize others.
- close with being genuine and appreciative.

At times we may want to round for a particular purpose. For example, the Estacada School District, Oregon deployed a leader rounding process when we worked with their leaders and instructional coaches to implement classroom improvement cycles in their classrooms with teachers. The leaders asked the instructional coaches, principals, and several teachers, what's working well with the classroom improvement cycles and why? What barriers are you facing with the classroom improvement cycles and why? Has anyone implemented the classroom improvement cycles really well? What did they do?

The second question we get is, "What if employees ask for things that we can't provide?" We've found that people ask for the simplest things. They may assume we know they are lacking resources, such as white board markers that don't work, lawn mower equipment that is in constant repair, or clocks in offices and rooms that need a new battery. We all have pet peeves that can get in the way of our work. Rounding with employees places us in front of these barriers. We are addressing roadblocks to productive work.

We hold Studer Education conferences throughout the year. At most conferences I deliver a presentation on stage. We have a standard practice at our events of being on time. That's a given and always occurs. We also have varying ways that we help people manage their time on stage. My pet need is that I like to have a timer in front of me. It's important for me to have this equipment so I can give my best to the audience. I get distracted when I look at my watch or phone or try to find where the timing signs are in the back of the room. It jeopardizes my commitment to the audience. I don't want to let them down. Mandy Gagliardi, who manages media at our events, knows this about me. I started asking about the timer every time we had an event. She always reassured me she had it covered and then asked me if I wanted to see what it looked like. She walked me to the stage to show me where the timer was. Prior to the conference she does a mini rounding with me. Does the setup work for you? Is there anything that would make it better? Let me know what I can do to help you.

Little things make a big difference. When we round with employees, we discover what people need and why it is important to them. Most of the time, people ask for items that help them serve others in a better way. That's what makes our profession a special one.

## Special Types of Leader Rounding Conversations

We coach leaders on two additional conversations I consider special types of rounding conversations with specific purposes. First, we hold 30- and 90- day conversations with new employees or those new to a position in our organization.

Second, it's more important than ever to re-recruit our high performers. Therefore, we want to hold deeper conversations with them to ensure they stay with us and have what they need to continue to be high performing.

*30-and 90- Day Conversations*

Have you ever had a job where you can't wait until the weekend? It can't get here fast enough. The night before going to work you feel completely miserable. And when you are working, you can't believe how long a given day feels to you.

Many of us have been there at least once in our lives and some of us are living this experience now. For me, once was enough. I graduated from Florida State University with a business degree in 1985. The unemployment rate was about 8%, improving from an all-time high of 10% in 1983. College placement counselors were telling us that we were entering a job market with one of the worst unemployment rates since World War I. Now I don't know about you, but that was not very uplifting. I was trying to get my first professional job. Graduating from college, I was eager to enter the workforce, learn from professionals, and leverage my skills. I left Tallahassee, Florida and moved to Atlanta to live with my lifelong best friend as I was looking for a job.

I landed my first salaried job in Atlanta, showed up for work, was given a manual to read for two days in an office, asked to shadow someone for two days, and then began working in the field on the 5th day. I remember the leader of the organization coming into my office the morning of the 5th day, patting me on the back and saying something like "You are ready now. Go get 'em." I entered that day with high anxiety. I just thought that was the way of the professional world. So, off I went.

Every day the job became more and more miserable. I felt trapped in the daily work and was anxious that if I quit, I would be a failure at my first professional job.

Within 90 or so days, I made a transition from my first job to another in a new company. At this second job I got lucky. One of the leaders of the company served as a mentor. He taught me a great deal – lessons I continue to apply today.

Bad workplaces negatively affect our lives in significant ways. Working for a bad leader multiplies that effect. It's important for leaders to prioritize the well-being and development of people they supervise. To do so, leaders need to get the first 30 to 90 days right. Similarly, the person hired needs to do the same as we describe in the next chapter, Principle 6 Be Accountable.

To set the stage for a new hire, hold 30-day and 90-day meetings. The 30- and 90- day meetings are additional check points during this important time of onboarding a new hire. When supervisors schedule monthly meetings with new hires, they reinforce that this type of meeting is "business as usual." Too often when leaders ask to meet with employees, they share bad news or identify a problem that needs to be corrected. When leaders call employees into the office, they begin to wonder if they've done something wrong. By letting employees know up-front that these meetings will be occurring, leaders can reduce that anxiety.

Years ago, when I was teaching high school, we had an odd configuration with offices in the school. All the math, language arts, and history teachers were in a big room with their own office cubicles. The room was located behind the front office and the principal's office. The principal's assistant would come back to our cubicle to tell us that the principal wanted to speak with us - these were the days before email. The dreaded day of being called to the principal's office appeared. Walking to his office, I heard this undertone of groans with a little laughter. When I walked out of the principal's office back to my desk, heads popped up from the cubicles asking me – *"What did he want?"* They expected to hear something bad. And they were hoping they were not next on his list.

Leaders need to be aware that their interactions with employees can be perceived in different ways than we perceive them. So, let's reduce anxiety by letting people know in advance that we will be holding 30- and 90-day meetings. Let them know why you have scheduled the meeting. Thirty and 90-day meetings are intended to be positive. Leaders learn about the new hires' experiences to ensure they have the best first 90 days on the job. Let the new hires know what to expect.

The leader extends an introduction to a 30-day meeting reinforcing this is going to be a positive meeting that helps the leader gain insight into the new hire's experiences over the first 30 days.

The 30 day meeting includes questions, like those below, that give leaders good information about the initial workplace experiences of new hires.

1. **How do we compare to what we said we would be like?**
   New hires enter our organizations with expectations they heard during the interview. We ask them how we are doing in line with what we said we would do.

2. **Tell me what you like. What is going well?**
   We want to engage in a positive conversation with new hires. Give them an opportunity to tell us something positive about their work.

3. **I noticed you came to us from ___. Are there things you did there that might be helpful to us?**
   When people come to us from other organizations, they rely on their past experiences to make sense of new ones. New hires may have good ideas about how we can do something better. What do we tend to do when new hires offer advice from their past experiences? We say, *"That was then, this is now – you don't work at that organization anymore. This is the way we do things here."* By asking this question, we may gain some best practices that worked in other places. When new hires offer a new idea or practice, we remain open to listen and learn. The worst thing we could do is tell the new hire how that wouldn't work here. We ask about that experience, probe for understanding, and listen.

4. **Is there anything here you are uncomfortable with?**
   According to a report by Jobvite, 34% of new hires leave because of an incident or bad experience that drove them away. We want new hires to tell us about their discomforts so that we can do something about a situation before it goes on for too long. We want to address issues head on.

5. **As your supervisor, how can I be helpful?**
   We want new hires to know we are here to help them be their best at work and achieve success.

On the 90th day, we suggest that leaders ask the same questions and also add another to the mix if we are hiring new people on our team.

6. **Is there anyone you know who might be a valuable addition to our team?**
   This question helps us add talent to our team. Some of our best hires are people who others have recognized as high performers. Of course, we only ask this question to new hires we want to continue to employ. Hopefully, we followed a process to make a good hiring decision. If we made a hiring mistake, refer to the information on holding critical conversations in Chapter 4.

New hires deserve the best from their leaders. Holding 30- and 90- day conversations show them we care about their success in our organization. They also help us identify and solve issues the new hire may be facing. Hiring new team members is critical to achieving organizational excellence.

*Stay Interviews*

A stay interview is an in-person meeting with a long-term, high-performing employee. The purpose of stay interviews is to uncover why high performers continue to work in our organization and what we can do to re-recruit them. Remember, a study by the New Teachers project found that when we lose a high performing teacher, we have a 1 in 11 chance of hiring another high performer.

Stay interviews with high performers may be one of the most important actions we commit to doing. The same rules we apply for leader rounding still apply for stay interviews. Start with something positive, determine what needs to be recognized, and uncover any barriers getting in the way of the person being a high performer. Here are some possible questions for doing stay interviews with your highest performers.

- What do you look forward to when you come to work each day?
- What keeps you working here?
- What would make your work experience even better?
- Who on our team would be the biggest loss for you when doing your job? Why?
- Who takes things off your plate?
- Who is proactive in getting work accomplished without your guidance? What do they do?
- If you could change something about your job, what would that be?
- What talents are not being used in your current role?
- What skill would you like to develop?
- What might tempt you to leave?
- Is there anything I can do to keep you from leaving?

We may not be able to meet the requests that come to us. But we'll do what we can to be helpful. It's better to know what's on our high performers' minds by asking. If we can't meet a certain request, maybe there's something else we can do. Our high performers will proactively help us negotiate a good outcome for them.

## Coaching in the Moment

People learn best when we provide great coaching. Coaching our teams establishes a culture of learning. We provide constant feedback at the time of need. We coach to reinforce positive observed behaviors and actions and identify where performance gaps exist. We engage in productive conversations to correct our course as quickly and smoothly as possible. To coach well we need to know how to provide feedback in ways that keep people motivated and change their behaviors.

We've found that employees tend to score a particular survey item lower than most - *"I receive feedback about my performance."* People tell us they want feedback to improve. I believe people when they say that. Because I believe most people want to learn how to get better. They want to achieve excellence. Here's what is important to remember. Giving feedback is a subjective judgment by the person giving the feedback. When people judge others, they do so from their own viewpoints and experiences, which may or may not be what is best for someone to hear. Also, when we receive feedback, it tugs on our emotions.

Few of us respond well to someone telling us what to do or how to fix ourselves. We tend to respond well when people communicate by focusing on observations made, learnings from past mistakes, and suggestions from their experiences that could help others get better. This feedback is most helpful when it occurs at the moment and with the right approach. That's what I mean by "coaching in the moment." Find something that someone is doing right and let them know. If someone needs to improve, let them know that as well. The way we coach people in that moment is critical to getting the best outcome.

Let's look at several examples comparing what we tend to say to what could be a better practice.

- We tend to say, *"Good Job!"* Instead, let's say, *"That's right – what you did right there. What was going through your mind when you did that?"*
- We tend to say, *"That didn't work."* Instead, let's say, *"When you did that it didn't feel right to me. I'd like to explore why."*
- We tend to say, *"You need to improve your communication skills."* Instead, let's say, *"As I listened to your presentation (or conversation),*

*here's exactly where you started to lose me. Can we back up?"*

- We tend to say, *"You need to have your classroom management procedures posted in your classroom."* Instead, let's say, *"When your students walked in the door, I felt they didn't know how to organize themselves to start the class. How do they know what to do?"*

In the examples, the coach is describing how the misstep felt to the coach or what the coach observed. The coach asks questions to initiate a productive conversation. Coaches listen and probe to better understand how someone can improve. Coaches want those they are coaching to come up with possible improvements as they challenge the individual to think more deeply about why something is occurring, what is making the negative situation occur, and how they can change their behaviors and actions to make the situation better.

As colleagues we can practice "coaching in the moment" conversations with each other to build trust among our teams. We want our teammates to feel heard and appreciated. Our goal is not to sell someone on our way of doing things. Rather, we stay curious to gain insight on why someone is taking specific actions. Others have points of view that can contribute to the team. We may have a different point of view. When we do, we may ask our teammates if they've thought about doing something in the way we've approached the challenge. We ask them what they think about that approach and if they have ideas for how to advance or modify the approach. When they are "coaching in the moment," they ask you to provide more information about your idea so they can understand it better. The combination of ideas is heard, processed, and used to make good decisions. Here's the point.

"Coaching in the moment" opens the door for us to learn from each other as we work as a team to solve daily challenges.

"Coaching in the moment" and leader rounding are key leadership tactics that influence individual performance. "Coaching in the moment" occurs as people perform their jobs. Leader rounding is a proactive way to gain insight from individuals. A special kind of rounding, 30- and 90- day conversations, build intentional connections with new hires or people new to a role. Stay interviews target our highest performing employees to re-recruit them on our teams.

## Chapter 5 Summary

Good coaching includes the tactics in this chapter. Considering it's difficult to retain teachers and staff, let's put employees at the center of our work. Here's an approach for how we connect with employees along the performance curve.

- **New Hires:** Round with them weekly. Hold a 30-day conversation with them. Then round with new hires every other week until 90 days. Hold a 90-day conversation with the new hire. Always coach in the moment. Extend these approaches throughout the first year if needed to give new hires confidence in their abilities to be successful. We want to provide our new hires with every opportunity to be successful. When we dismiss new hires within the first year, we've made a bad hiring decision – that responsibility is on us.
- **High Performers:** Hold stay interviews with them every two months. Mix up the questions to stay connected with them and ask them if the organization is at risk of losing them. Always coach in the moment focusing on their high performing

behaviors to reinforce their value. Ask high performers what they want to work on and how you can help.

- **Solid Performers**: Round with them every 4 to 6 weeks. Always coach in the moment, doing it often. Spend the needed time with them to help them shift their performance up.
- **Low performers:** Round with them every 4 to 6 weeks but start with high and solid performers first. By doing so the low performers have a chance to see the positive effect rounding has on others. If rounding takes a turn and becomes negative stop the rounding session. Ask them to schedule a time with you to address the issues at hand. Put the ball back in their court to schedule the meeting. If poor performance continues hold critical conversations with them that were outlined in Chapter 4. Always coach in the moment and pay attention to how they respond.

Connecting with people shows we care. Remember our goal is to improve individual and organizational performance with more consistency. That only occurs when we attend to what's most important to people. We need to engage in meaningful conversations to know.

Principle 5 Focus on Employee Engagement puts people at the center of our work. An employee's experience in the workplace factors into organizational excellence. It's difficult, if not impossible, to achieve our goals without an engaged, skilled, and productive workforce. We expect people to come to work being accountable (Principle 6) for their behaviors and actions. We expect employees to be good organizational citizens. For that to occur, we owe them an inspiring workplace environment to be at their best.

# 6

# BE ACCOUNTABLE

*Commit to individual accountability to achieve organizational goals.*

Principle 6 Be Accountable focuses on how to create a sense of ownership within the organization. Our goal as leaders is to support a culture where people feel ownership for their actions. We want to activate the will of our employees to contribute in particular ways that benefit the organization. This is different from employees feeling motivated. Leaders can't motivate employees. Employees motivate themselves. Leaders can create a culture where people are inspired to motivate themselves. And where leaders avoid words and actions that discourage people.

Most important, we want to create workplaces where people have a deep connection to the work and a motivating force that drives them toward accomplishing their work at a deeper level. That's what is meant by employees being owners of their work. Employees come to work living the organizational values, engaging with their teams, accomplishing organizational goals, and consistently being at their best.

Leaders in positions model what they expect of their employees. To have strong organizations, these leaders must be high performing leaders. Holding a leadership position is a choice people make. This choice requires leaders to be accountable to others and to the organizational goals. By doing so, leaders in positions empower their employees to lead. When we have good leadership across the board, our organizations thrive. People in the organization are committed to creating inspiring workplaces, building strength in people, and accelerating results. Being accountable has a direct link to creating workplace environments where people have purpose, do worthwhile work, and make a difference.

A critical barrier for creating inspiring workplaces is incivility in the workplace. Leaders must hold individuals accountable for being uncivil to others, including their team members and "customers." Some forms of incivility are overt, like insulting people, being rude, and continuously blaming someone for problems. To be accountable leaders, we simply can't tolerate this behavior from our employees. We move quickly to holding critical conversations with uncivil employees to address the damaging behaviors. Uncivil behavior can also be more subtle, like people emailing or doing other work at a meeting, teasing people with underhanded jabs, interrupting others, giving someone a dirty look, and having side conversations at meetings. An expert in civility, Christine Porath, claims that such seemingly minor acts can be as harmful as overt uncivil behaviors, because they are less obvious and easier to overlook, yet they add up eventually eroding the workplace spirit.

In a study across multiple industries, Porath's team found several salient findings among workers who had been on the receiving end of incivility.

- 48% intentionally decreased their work effort.
- 47% intentionally decreased the time spent at work.
- 38% intentionally decreased the quality of their work.
- 80% lost work time worrying about the incident.

- 63% lost work time avoiding the offender.
- 66% said that their performance declined.
- 78% said that their commitment to the organization declined.
- 12% said that they left their job because of the uncivil treatment.
- 25% admitted to taking their frustration out on customers.

To be accountable leaders we must be vigilant about keeping the workplace civil. One uncivil action multiplies to more negative interactions creeping into the workplace until it begins to shape an unhealthy culture. As leaders, we need to keep our own behaviors in check. How we come across to others sets the tone for fostering civility in our organization.

Dr. Beverly Walker-Griffea is the President of Mott Community College in Flint, Michigan. She has been a long-time advocate for collegiate student success, serving community college students in various capacities for more than 30 years. Dr. Beverly, as she prefers to be called, has a passion for ensuring all students have access to quality, affordable, and effective learning experiences. She is highly committed to a community that has experienced extreme struggles over many decades.

We have the great fortune of working with Dr. Beverly and her team to apply the Nine Principles Framework. Dr. Beverly's focus on civility as part of their strategic plan has helped me understand how important Principle 6 is for leaders to follow. Civility is a core belief in the Mott Community College Strategic Plan. Dr. Beverly took one step further. She immersed the employees, leaders, and Board of Trustees in the realities of the Flint community leading to the adoption of a civility policy by the MCC board. The policy reads, *"Mott Community College encourages and promotes an environment of civility and mutual respect among its diverse employees and student body. Faculty, staff, and students should treat one another in a respectful manner with civility, honesty, and courtesy. Each individual is expected to have regard for the dignity and needs of the people with whom they work and interact. Employees and students are reminded that freedom of expression comes with a responsibility to respect the rights and reputations of others."* This is not simply a policy on the books; it is active everywhere on campus. Dr. Beverly holds herself and the Mott leaders accountable for being civil to each other, students, their families, and the community. For example, in the leadership development institutes we hold with the core leaders, we include positive examples of team members demonstrating civility on campus. Dr. Beverly also includes questions about this core belief in her leader rounding sessions with employees. She listens and brings concerns forward to her leadership team to solve.

Being a good citizen in our organization means we are civil to each other and our "customers." One uncivil incident spreads to another, which comes with the cost of losing good employees, students and families who depend on us, and respect from the communities we serve.

## Start with Facing the Brutal Facts

Over the years, I've worked on developing the concepts, tools and tactics aligned to this principle more than any others from the original inception of the principles focused on the healthcare profession. Here's why. When organizations see a momentum shift in a negative direction, it's usually related to this standard. It's a very difficult one to coach because leaders, including me, tend to struggle with looking in the mirror when things start going south. I don't know about you, but I seem to have a love - hate relationship with being accountable. When we think of being accountable, we may think of something negative, like being penalized for not achieving our goals or making a mistake with a "customer" and being embarrassed. We may start to wonder if we are good enough for our positions. Even so, we must persevere by looking at the "brutal facts" and learning how we can improve.

In *Good to Great*, Jim Collins uses the term "brutal facts" to describe the need for leaders to confront the realities of their organizations. He says, *"Leadership does not begin with just a vision. It begins with getting people to confront the brutal facts and act on the implications."*

Collins shares that every good to great company faced adversity along the way to greatness. They achieved greatness by maintaining an unwavering faith in the endgame, and a commitment to prevail to achieve goals despite the brutal facts that were in front of them. Collins called this duality the Stockdale Paradox.

The name refers to Admiral Jim Stockdale, who was the highest-ranking United States military officer in a prisoner-of-war camp during the height of the Vietnam War. Tortured over twenty times during his eight-year imprisonment from 1965 to 1973, Stockdale lived out the war without any prisoner's rights, no set release date, and no certainty as to whether he would even survive to see his family again.

Collins and one of his graduate students had lunch with Stockdale. Collins wanted to know how Stockdale dealt with such a bleak situation of uncertainty of survival to make it out.

Stockdale said, *"I never lost faith in the end of the story, I never doubted not only that I would get out, but also that I would prevail in the end and turn the experience into the defining event of my life, which, in retrospect, I would not trade."*

Collins asked Stockdale, *"Who didn't make it out?"* Stockdale said, *"That's easy – the optimists. They were the ones who said, 'We're going to be out by Christmas.' And Christmas would come, and Christmas would go. Then they'd say, 'We're going to be out by Easter.' And Easter would come, and Easter would go. And then Thanksgiving, and then it would be Christmas again. And they died of a broken heart."*

Stockdale continued, *"This is a very important lesson. You must never confuse faith that you will prevail in the end, which you can never afford to lose, with the discipline to confront the most brutal facts of your current reality, whatever they might be."*

Sometimes, we believe our actions will produce positive outcomes, yet the results go awry. What does the Stockdale Paradox teach us? Facing the brutal facts will help us prevail. To do so, we commit to being accountable to ourselves, our employees, our students and families, and our communities. We welcome accountability for being a good citizen in our organization and leading with perseverance by facing the realities that are in front of us head on.

This chapter is about what it takes to be an accountable member of an organization. It links being accountable to the Standards of Excellence, describes the characteristics of employees being owners of their work, and reinforces the significance of hiring people who align to the organizational culture.

## Connecting to Our Standards of Excellence

Unless we determine what's acceptable and what's not, it's difficult for people to know how to be accountable. The Standards of Excellence described in Chapter 1 are designed through a collaborative process to spell out the behaviors we expect individuals to exhibit at work. The standards address how we interact with our colleagues and our customers. It's what we all agree to live by when we are working together. The standards clearly communicate how employees are expected to act and what the boundaries are.

The Standards of Excellence define workplace expectations. Individual accountability occurs when people are living the standards at work. At times people fail to live the standards. They may check themselves, admit their mistake, apologize to their team, and change their behavior. At other times, peers can help each other. Peers can recognize their team members when they are living the standards and provide friendly checks when they are not.

Our tendency is to look for what's wrong even when we know there's a lot that is going right. Our Standards of Excellence help teams recognize each other. To do so, all employees need to know and live by the standards. One of our coaches, Dr. KK Owen, shared an example of peer recognition. Someone in her service excellence training session saw a great example of a coworker living one of the organizational standards. The coworker was engaging in a conversation with an angry parent. This is what she said to her co-worker, *"Wow-you did a really good job with that parent just now. You remained calm, you listened with empathy to her story, and you remembered to ask her what she thought the best solution might be-just like we learned it in our service excellence training!"*

Everyone in the organization can recognize others for living the standards. Recognition from leaders is important. Recognition from our peers is sometimes even more important. As you'll hear us say time and again, *what gets recognized gets repeated*. And, when we hear this in one-on-one conversations with our peers, it makes us feel good.

In Chapter 1, I provided an example of Northwestern Illinois Association's Standards of Excellence. Jon Malone, the Executive Leader, created a system of peer recognition. He created a portal that any employee can use to recognize a team member at any time. The results are published monthly for the entire organization. I've seen Jon and his team present their standards, how they apply them, and the positive results that have occurred in his organization. This process serves as the foundation for building a positive workplace culture. His team knows exactly how to be accountable.

At Studer Education we developed our Standards of Excellence that continue to be updated over time. At our quarterly strategy sessions, we engage in activities that reinforce the expectations outlined in our standards. Here's an example. Our engagement team reviewed the standards with us that included the name of the standard, the definition, and descriptors for each standard. We all received a puzzle piece made of paper. On one side we placed the standard that resonated with us the most and on the other side we wrote a word or phrase for how the standard connected to us. We rotated around the room describing our puzzle pieces and then placed them on the floor connecting them to another puzzle piece aligned to our four Standards of Excellence. At the end of the session, we had created a team puzzle on the floor that remained with us throughout our two days together. Walking by the puzzle we were reminded of what we expect of ourselves and our colleagues.

We want people to be individually accountable for their actions and behaviors. The Standards of Excellence set common expectations that are defined by employees.

Therefore, they own their behaviors and strive to be accountable.

## Being an Owner of Your Work

I refer to owners as those who see themselves as co-owners of the organizational mission and goals. They develop a sense of individual accountability to see that things get done at the highest levels of performance. Owners strive for excellence as part of their personal and professional continuous improvement process.

Accountable people are **excellent team members** and **contribute to the success** of the organization. What does individual accountability look like when people are collaboratively working as an **excellent team**? Accountable individuals

- care about what is occurring around them.
- understand their jobs and responsibilities.
- aren't waiting for someone to tell them what to do.
- are willing to help others.
- earn the respect of others.
- work together for the common good.
- take responsibility for their career path.

I find this last characteristic of an excellent team member to be especially valuable. Owners of their work don't expect leaders to pave a path for them to progress in the organization. Rather owners assume new responsibilities to develop their skills that may position them for advanced positions. Individuals who take the initiative usually position themselves to lead their teams.

One of our team members offers a great example for others to follow. Years ago, we hired Mandy Gagliardi on a temporary, part-time basis to help us enter survey data. As she listened and engaged with our team, she heard us talking about the need to create a one-page solution description document. She offered to help. What we learned is that Mandy was a talented graphic artist with great connections to our team. Mandy also had technology systems skills and offered help to anyone in need. Our team started to count on Mandy as part of our team. We hired Mandy full-time. She continued to learn, grow, and develop. She never expects anyone to pave the path for her. She paved her own path and is now a key, trusted leader on our team. I recall a time when I sent a text to Mandy when I awoke one morning. It said, *"Please tell me you aren't leaving our team. I had a nightmare that you were taking a job elsewhere."* Now, that's when you know someone is a high performer!

Another key leader on our team who started with us on a part-time basis is Tatiana Keith. She joined us as a part-time field placement advisor for TeacherReady. She did that job so well we hired her full-time. Now she serves as key leader on our team and is continuing to advance in our organization. Tatiana models the team excellence characteristics described above. Tatiana doesn't wait for someone to tell her what to do. She recognizes a problem or need and inserts her expertise to lead others on the team. I also know I can count on Tatiana to do the deep work to achieve the goals. She contributes to the overall success of our organization by being an owner of her work.

Like Tatiana and Mandy, accountable individuals also contribute to the **success of the organization**. They

- connect the dots between what they do and the strategic direction and goals of the organization.
- engage in conversations to seek solutions as problems arise.

- assume necessary responsibilities to accomplish goals.
- follow-up to make sure nothing gets dropped.
- prioritize their work aligned to the goals.
- make things happen.
- act in ways that demonstrate we can count on them.

The Standards of Excellence define what high performing behaviors look like in our organizations. The bulleted items on **building team excellence** and **contributing to organizational success** serve as learning outcomes for professionally developing people to be accountable. This type of development makes becoming an owner a natural part of work.

Here's an important note. People who are in leadership positions must model how to be accountable. According to the Global Leadership Accountability Study, 72% of employees believe leadership accountability is a critical business issue, and 31% are satisfied with the degree of leadership accountability in their organization. The results show how important it is for leaders to master the learning outcomes presented above.

Employees are watching what their leaders do. For example, they watch to see if leaders are living the Standards of Excellence and following through with their promises. They watch to see how leaders react to difficult decisions. At those times when leaders make a mistake or fail to act in ways that align to cultural expectations, it's important for them to openly acknowledge the misstep and sincerely apologize.

One common way I've seen leaders stray from living the organizational values links to how they use their mobile devices. It's easy to get caught up with constantly looking at our phones. Doing so while being with others indicates we do not value someone's time. As we've shifted to virtual interactions, I've noticed that people put their pictures on camera while doing other work. I don't know about you, but it's evident when people are staring expressionless at the camera. They don't have negative intent; they get caught up in what's most important to them. If we've been guilty of behaviors like this, let's apologize to our team and stop doing them. Let's turn our full attention to others when they have the floor. That's what accountable people do – they show others that they care about who they are and what they can contribute to the team.

You hear us say, *what we permit, we promote*. If we permit anyone in our organization to live outside of the standards, our actions say that it's ok to do that. Negative actions jeopardize building a positive culture. On the other hand, when we consistently recognize people for living the organizational standards, we reinforce how valuable people are and how being accountable is part of building an inspiring workplace.

Prior to learning about the Nine Principles Framework, I had moments as a leader where I failed to be accountable. I remember a time when I was leading a small committee to accomplish a big organizational task. The members on the committee had been long-standing, good colleagues of mine. The senior administration placed their confidence in me to lead this work. Prior to starting the meeting, I used the time as a platform to complain about things in the organization that were presenting barriers for me to lead. After several sessions, one of my colleagues asked me if I ever had anything positive to say about the organization. It caught me off guard. Addressing my negative behavior took courage. After the meeting I went to her office and thanked her for calling me out. I was not accountable for my own behavior. From that point on, I stopped opening the meeting with complaints, but the damage was done to my colleagues. To correct that I needed to own my mistake in front of them by apologizing to the group. We are going to make mistakes. When we do let's own our negative behaviors, stop them from occurring, and apologize to others who have been affected by our actions.

## Hiring People Who Align to Our Culture

Individual accountability starts on the first day of a job for new employees. Therefore, it's important that we hire the right people who fit the organizational culture. We want to give new hires every opportunity to deeply connect to the work. To hire the right people, we design job descriptions aligned to job competencies rather than job tasks. We include competencies aligned to the job and Standards of Excellence to assess the cultural fit. We share our Standards of Excellence with new employees and ask interview questions aligned to the standards as well as to their job responsibilities.

In the interviews, we want to know how a candidate would handle certain situations. The Standards of Excellence can be used to create workplace situations focused on individual accountability. The response by the candidate gives us a way to assess the cultural fit of the candidate. We don't want people to leave the interview without understanding how well they align to the organizational culture. I've found that most people who struggle in new positions don't align their behaviors to what is expected. When organizations develop the standards and use them to hire people, new hires can hit the ground running. Prior to hiring new employees, we ask them to sign the Standards of Excellence, agreeing to live with the stated workplace expectations.

As soon as the job is accepted, we reach out to the new hire with a nice welcome note or call. We want to stay engaged with them between the window of accepting the job to the first day on the job.

We start new hires off on the right foot by

- openly welcoming them to our team.
- showing how appreciative we are that they chose to be on our team.
- providing well-defined onboard training.
- connecting them to our mission, values, strategic direction, and goals.
- showing them how their job responsibilities align to the goals.
- providing solid training on the Standards of Excellence.
- showcasing the skills they bring to our team.

Starting on day one we touch base with the new hire letting them know that we are here to support them to be successful. During the first 90 days, we hold rounding and 30- and 90- day conversations with our new hires, and we intentionally connect with them often. We described these tactics in Chapter 5.

The best leaders hire the right people and support them to have a successful first 90 days. According to a report by Jobvite, about 30% of new hires quit their jobs within the first 90 days. Forty-three percent say that their role doesn't meet the expectations that had been set for them, 34% report that a specific incident drove them away, and 32% blame company culture. Most people want to work for an excellent organization where leaders and their teammates are accountable. If that doesn't occur, we may lose some highly talented and valuable people. Therefore, it's important to train and expect employees to align their behaviors to the Standards of Excellence. It's equally important to hire people who are excited and skilled to work in an organization that adheres to living the standards and reinforcing a positive culture.

## Chapter 6 Summary

Principle 6 Be Accountable means we commit to individual accountability to achieve the organizational goals. We want to be that person that others can rely on. We want to be able to rely on others. To do so, we live the Standards of Excellence, we act as co-owners of our organizations, and we hire people who have the skills to do the job and are a cultural fit. Remember, it's critical for leaders to model these behaviors for their teams. Only then can we expect employees to be accountable for their behaviors and actions at work.

We have an opportunity to work with executive leaders who understand how important individual accountability is to the success of the organization. Equally so, they know they must be accountable executive leaders.

When I think of leaders that go first and model the way for 'what right looks like,' I think of Rob Clayton, Superintendent of Warren County Public Schools (WCPS) in Kentucky. In 2016, Rob went first and became the first Kentucky public school district to partner with Studer Education. We've grown to serving 16 school districts in Kentucky and look forward to serving more.

In July 2022, Rob was selected as the 2023 Kentucky Superintendent of the Year by the Kentucky Association of School Administrators and recently afterward, he was named the 2022 National Superintendent of the Year by the National

Association of School Superintendents. In Rob's press release he stated, *"If you're going to continue to move forward and not become stagnant, you need outstanding leaders throughout the organization. That's our focus and it won't change."* Rob expects excellence from all his leaders in building an inspiring workplace and applying excellent service. The consistently high district survey results on employee engagement and internal service excellence demonstrate his commitment to applying aligned leadership practices throughout the school district.

Here's how Rob holds himself accountable to ensure the district's mission and vision come to life on behalf of all students. He recognizes the importance of surrounding himself with a great team of people. He leads with an intentional focus on developing leaders at all levels of the organization. Here are several key actions that show his focus.

- Each leader sets goals on their Professional Growth Plan that include their Studer Action Plan Goals from their Employee Engagement Survey and their Studer Survey results reflected on their school and district scorecards. This drives the positive organizational culture within each of their 25 schools and central office departments. Accountability begins with the leader which is a consistent focus in their district's improvement process.
- Rob serves as the chair of each principal selection committee. In addition, throughout their first year, Rob supports all new principals as their primary evaluator. His personal involvement with new leaders reflects his strong desire to ensure each principal is the right fit for the organization and the organization is the right fit for them. New leaders are also served directly by members of the executive

leadership team which works to ensure each new leader embraces and internalizes the vision. Finally, new leaders are supported through a year-long onboarding program/new leader academy.

In addition to a high focus on developing leaders, Rob sees communication as a big part of being accountable. He believes decision-making begins with listening and ensuring the right people are seated at the table prior to making significant decisions. He leads his executive team to build ownership and commitment by

- listening, soliciting input, and checking for understanding.
- delivering clear, concise, consistent, and cascaded messages.
- identifying unintended consequences from decisions early on by bringing tough issues to the table to solve in a collaborative way.
- holding consistent leadership huddles to get in front of challenging decisions.
- engaging with business partners and the community in intentional ways to gain insights and share ideas.

Rob has demonstrated that the strength of an extraordinary district is directly aligned to growing the leadership capacity of administrators and employees at all organizational levels. And Rob is an accountable leader holding his executive team and all district leaders to high expectations while supporting them to be at their best.

It's nearly impossible to create inspiring workplaces that build strength in people to accelerate results without executive leaders like Rob demonstrating accountable behaviors for all leaders and employees to follow. As an executive leader, I remind myself of this every day, knowing that my every action holds me accountable to those I serve. I need to make sure the needs of others are met and know my actions will always speak louder than my words.

# 7

# ALIGN BEHAVIORS WITH GOALS AND VALUES

*Apply consistent practices to move the organization in a positive direction.*

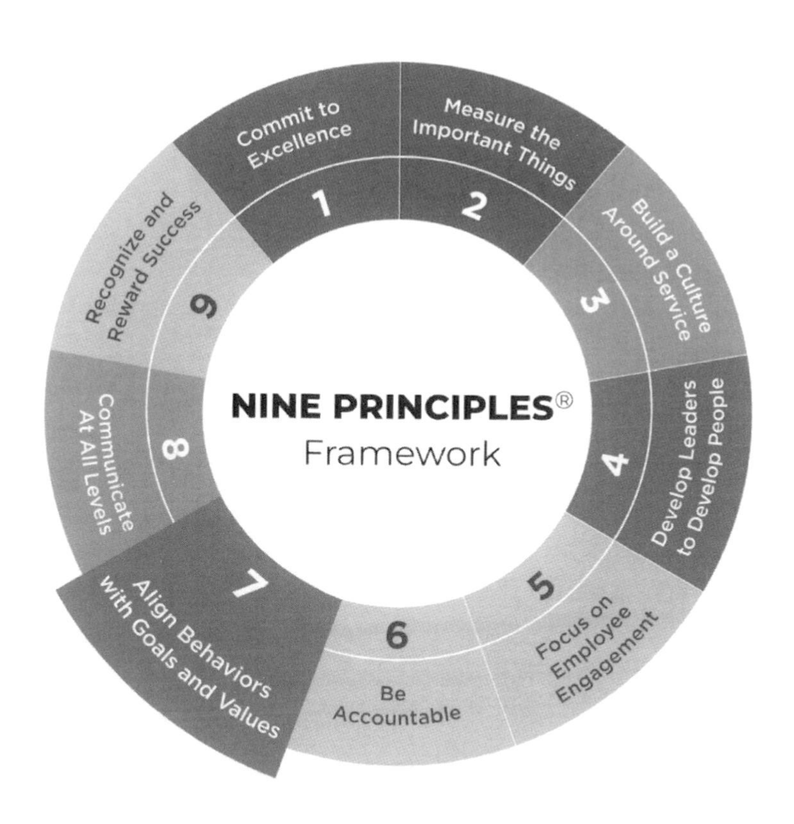

Aligning our behaviors with goals and values relies on people having an improvement mindset described in Chapter 1. We strive to achieve measurable goals and tackle any challenges that come our way, always knowing we can get better and better at our craft. To improve continuously, we need to challenge people to up their game to assume the challenges that make the organization better.

One of the biggest challenges is knowing when to push people and when to pull back. We improve when we experience enough discomfort to help us grow. Think about what it feels like to learn something new. We are excited yet anxious that we may fail. It's much more comfortable to stay at the level where we are comfortable. To improve our skills, we must move through our discomfort to get to the other side. Continuous improvement is about assuming continuous challenges to get better and better.

During the pandemic, I bought a Class A motorhome. It's 34 feet long. It's the first time I've owned an RV of any kind. There's so much to learn. The RV instructors provide a speed course on all you need to know. Then, it's yours to manage, fresh off the lot. I was excited and anxious. I elected to spend the first year camping close to home. I needed to learn how to work all the parts that made for a great camping experience. The first several times, I was uncomfortable and hit some roadblocks.

I wanted to sell it back! I loved the camping experience, so I worked through the discomfort. The more I practiced the better I got. I gained confidence as certain procedures became second nature. It's a continuous learning journey!

This place of discomfort is what Peter Senge calls creative tension. It is the pressure point between the way things could be and the way things are. Think of pulling a rubber band - the tighter we pull the more pressure or tension we create. If we don't pull tight enough, we don't have enough tension to create the urgency to improve. We will see little to no improvement. Pulling the rubber band too tight creates extreme tension causing stress and burnout.

In his historical best-selling book, *The Fifth Discipline*, Peter Senge tells us that high performing organizations maintain a felt sense of creative tension. It's a source of energy. We learn and grow when we feel challenged. That's how we get better.

Too little creative tension causes the organization to feel flat, compliant, and lethargic. Too much creative tension causes a sense of anxiousness causing people to give up or not see a way to achieve a goal. If leaders fail to master the ability to lead and manage creative tension, a constrained and entrenched organizational culture will overpower the leader. Our leadership jobs depend on how well we lead and manage creative tension.

Pressure can be positive – the right amount of pressure. On the other hand, continued and overburdening stress is not positive. When the level of pressure is right for the work we are doing, we are excited and engaged in our work. If we feel like things are out of control in our work environment, we may raise the white flag and surrender. It's beyond what we see as practical and reasonable. We don't see how what we are doing contributes to something of value. It feels as if more is added to our plates.

Have you ever left a meeting feeling overwhelmed, like one more thing was added to your plate? You didn't know why, understand the value, or see how it connects to the larger picture. You wonder if the person leading the meeting remembered the other things added to your plate at the last meeting, and the meeting before that, and the meeting before that one. We're good at doing new things and not so good at stopping what we are doing that's not working. That's the plate filler.

Recently I was talking with a new leader. He said that he was feeling overwhelmed. I asked why that was the case. He said things in the organization seemed chaotic. People were working hard. He couldn't put his finger on how the work was contributing to something worthwhile. He said, we just keep swirling and more gets added to the plate. Everything seemed urgent. John Kotter calls this issue false urgency in organizations. He compares what work looks like when leaders lead with a false sense of urgency versus the right urgency. We are striving to place the right amount and type of urgency in our organizations to manage through the discomfort of being challenged.

Kotter says living with a false sense of urgency shows up in the work environment in the following ways.

- frantic, chaotic, and disconnected activity
- lack of aligned actions to outcomes
- meetings to address all issues
- projects grow without understanding how they fit into the organization
- high stress levels
- passive aggressive behaviors
- so much work to be done that it feels like we are always being pushed to the limit

Feeling this way, people shift from being a team player to someone finding a way to stay motivated. Leaders work in silos controlling and managing what they can.

Kotter recommends we lead with the right sense of urgency by taking the following actions.

- Set challenging yet achievable measurable goals.
- Align sub-unit measures to organizational results.
- Build transparency of results with the organization.
- Address underperforming data head on and move to action to improve.
- Put more honest discussions in organizational communication.
- Eliminate excess and focus on high levels of productivity.

The Nine Principles Framework offers tools and tactics for leaders to lead with the right sense of urgency.

As I've gotten older, I'm less tolerant of unproductive demands that add stress. But I'm eager to strive for goals that add the right amount of pressure to stay motivated. I bet this sounds familiar. That's what Principle 7 Align Behaviors with Goals and Values is all about. The leadership tactics in this chapter help us live on the right side of the urgency that Kotter describes.

## Connecting Creative Tension to the Elephant and the Rider

As I describe the tactics in this chapter, picture how they help us pull and release the rubber band to lead with the right amount of tension. Also, keep the picture of the elephant and the rider in your mind that was introduced earlier in the book. It's a picture of a big elephant with a small rider traveling a path and mapping out new paths as they travel down the road. The Rider is rational and can therefore see a path ahead. While underneath him, the Elephant provides the power for the journey. The Elephant represents the emotional part of the organization. The rider might know where to go but needs to encourage the elephant to move forward.

Many of the chapters in this book focus on the elephant. The rider is unable to travel the journey without the elephant. That's how important nurturing the elephant is. This chapter focuses on the rider – what it takes to create a clear path and how to know when to adjust the path during the travels to achieve goals.

To travel the path and shape it as we go, the rider and elephant need to travel together. The rider holds the reigns but can be completely overmatched if they disagree about the direction. Leading with the right tension is critical to shaping the path for the rider and the elephant to travel together.

When we lead with and manage with the right amount of tension (knowing when to pull and loosen the rubber band) we tap into individual creativity and ideas to help our organizations achieve better outcomes. We feel a sense of excitement. We know how to manage with the right amount of pressure to build productive energy among our teams. Let's take a deeper look at the tools and tactics leaders use to align the right behaviors with the goals and values to achieve results.

Senior leaders set the strategic vision and direction of the organization. They answer the questions, What does our organization want to become? How will our organization remain relevant? How does our organization serve our students and families and become a cornerstone of our communities? Ten years out, what will we look like if we are successful and how will we know? The answers build the framework for designing the organization's strategic plan.

The strategic planning process includes input from multiple audiences in line with the strategic vision and direction. Once the strategic plan is developed, leaders use a scorecard process to execute the plan. The scorecard includes the measures that define success. The strategic planning process was described in Chapter 1 and the design of the organizational scorecard was described in Chapter 2.

I have the pleasure of working with Ysleta Independent School District (YISD) in El Paso, Texas. Dr. Xavier De La Torre, one of our Difference Maker Award recipients, is the superintendent and is surrounded by a talented executive leadership team. YISD has about 39,000 students, 94% of YISDs student body is Hispanic and about 80% are from low-income families. The community is highly committed to the schools and has shown that commitment by passing two significant bonds over the past decade to support the schools.

As we began our work together, we held input sessions with employees, parents, students, and community members. The community is highly invested in the school district and appreciated the opportunity to provide input to the superintendent, executive team, and school board. The leadership and board listened to the voices of the people and designed a strategic plan that continues to evolve and grow as the Ysleta Independent School District advances. We then worked with the board and Dr. De La Torre to establish the district scorecard that serves as the key tool for the board evaluating the superintendent's annual performance. This keeps both the board and leadership team aligned and focused on the agreed upon goals. The leadership team continues to gain input from the various groups by administering employee, family, and service excellence surveys and applying the survey roll out process described in this book. Using key strategies and behaviors aligned to measurable goals, YISD has achieved the designation of an "A" District in the state of Texas.

In YISD and other partner organizations, the strategic plan provides the framework for determining the "winning moves" for doing the work that matters to achieve positive results. The scorecard includes the organizational measures that define success. It's now time to align behaviors, actions, and processes to achieve the goals. This alignment shapes the path the elephant and the rider travel together. That's what our high performing partner organizations like the Ysleta Independent School District do to achieve excellence.

How do leaders align behaviors with goals and values to travel and shape the organizational path? People need to know the current realities of their organizations; what they are trying to accomplish, how the organizational goals align to their units, and how what they do contributes to the success of the organization. Organizational leaders need to see a path to accomplish their goals. It's here where leaders outline the direction and engage people in a continuous improvement approach to know where the bright spots are, where the gaps are, and how to improve. Applying a continuous improvement approach involves people in shaping and re-shaping the path.

In summary, an improvement approach requires solid execution and alignment throughout all units in our organizations. We apply an iterative and continuous process that answers these questions.

- What are we trying to accomplish?
- What results are we trying to achieve?
- How do we continuously review where we are so that we know what to keep doing, stop doing, and adjust what we are doing?

- What changes can we make that will result in improvements?
- How do we apply a system to continuously review how we are doing in areas that are most critical to organizational success?

Let's now focus on how we use the organizational measures and strategies to align our behaviors to achieve results by meeting our goals and honoring our values.

## Cascade and Align Key Measures and Strategic Actions

As indicated, leaders influence the strategic direction for achieving results. Equally as important, they are accountable for executing the strategic plan and priorities. I often rely on the concepts– people first, service is everything, strategy equals execution, and results matter. As we've summarized, leaders depend on people to execute a strategic direction. Our ability to serve each other and our "customers" is a must have, not a nice to have. We specifically focused on people in Chapter 4 and 5, service excellence in Chapter 3, and strategy in Chapter 1. In this chapter, we focus on strategic execution and alignment. The scorecard process described in Chapter 2 lays the groundwork for leaders to execute the plan. The process includes

- key organizational results measures that define success.
- aligned progress monitoring measures.
- focused strategic actions that have the highest impact on results.

Dr. Kathy Oropallo, one of our leader coaches, shared a typical example of a district applying the scorecard process for the parent pillar. After reviewing the parent satisfaction results the leaders identified a core problem. More than half of the parents in the district didn't feel welcomed or respected at their respective schools. During the roll-out process at the schools, the following potential causes of the problems were identified: busy office staff, no consistent or clear expectations for how parents are welcomed at schools, and language barriers for staff and families. Here is an example of a scorecard (Figure 11) for one annual measure with accompanying progress measures and key actions for a school district.

| ANNUAL MEASURE | PROGRESS MEASURES | KEY ACTIONS |
|---|---|---|
| Bi-Annual mean results for family survey items 4,7,13,14 | FAMILY SURVEY: Pulse checks every 75 days<br><br>4. My family is treated with respect at this school.<br>7. I would recommend this school to other parents.<br>13. I receive positive phone calls, emails, or notes about my child from the school.<br>14. The principal at this school is approachable and reachable. | Hardwire AIDET and service excellence strategies across all schools.<br><br>Provide support for front line staff with options for language barriers. |

*Figure 11. Scorecard for Annual Measures on Family Survey*

Our work focuses on districts and focuses on single schools or feeder patterns of schools. Here's an example from Erwin Middle School in Jefferson County School District, Alabama of aligning annual measures, progress measures, and key actions for a school. (Figure 12). This example focuses on the student achievement pillar for the school. Dr. Angela

Bush is the principal of the school. Erwin Middle school was considered a "failing school." Over the years, we've had the pleasure of working alongside Dr. Bush to continuously improve results. The school now serves as a model school for moving results up (even during the two years of the pandemic). We constantly showcase Dr. Bush's leadership and the work being accomplished in the school as some of the best performance results in the country.

| ANNUAL MEASURE | PROGRESS MEASURES | KEY ACTIONS |
|---|---|---|
| To achieve 80% attendance rate for all students.<br>To achieve a B or better average for all students. | Weekly, bi-weekly attendance and tardy data. (Reported out on 30-60-90 day cycles.)<br>Bi-weekly student average data. (Reported out on 30-60-90 day cycles.) | Hire a new counselor to serve as liaison between EMS school and EMS parents/ students.<br>Pull list of students with "D" and "F" averages. Provide new counselor with attendance report<br>Assigned counselors. One will be in constant communication with teachers and attend weekly PLCs to update teachers on the status of their students whose families he has contacted. Teachers will keep track of their remote absence using a common google form. The other counselor will be in constant communication with EMS parents and students to identify barriers that are hindering students from being present (Both traditionally and remotely) at school. |

*Figure 12. School Scorecard for Student Achievement Measures*

To execute a district strategic plan well, we apply a scorecard process to determine the measures that matter with aligned actions to achieve the goals across all schools and departments. At a system level, once an organization has a scorecard in place and is successfully implementing the process at one level, it's time to cascade the process to other units. The scorecard process guides leaders, teachers, and staff on the outcomes they are trying to achieve, the measures they use to track their progress, and the key actions they apply to achieve the results. School and department teams understand what they are working on and how what they are doing aligns to the organizational goals. Let's review an example of district scorecard goals cascading to a department.

Rick Fechter is a high performing operational facilities leader in the School District of Menomonee Falls, Wisconsin. The school district scorecard goal was to reduce operational costs by a certain amount. Rick's team focused on reducing costs so that the savings could be reallocated to student learning. The facilities division had measurable goals on their scorecard aligned to the district goal focused on reduction of worker compensation costs. The division scorecard goals included measures associated with custodial cleaning quality, snow removal, and grass cutting. Here were the results that occurred.

- Reduced workers comp cost from $300,000 to $12,970 (over 4 years)
- Improved custodial cleaning quality levels from 3.65 to 3.83 in one year that equaled annual savings of $140,000
- Saved $40,000 a year on snow removal costs
- District Grass Cutting Program
    - Eliminated two grounds summer team workers at a savings of $10,000 per year

- o Grounds team improved speed of grass cutting by 2.5 days equaling a 50% reduction in labor time in that area that could be re-positioned to increase efficiencies in the department

Rick guided his team to see how their work impacted the overall district goal. His team was also motivated to execute with quality knowing the cost reduction has a direct impact on the dollars that could be reallocated in the classroom.

For Rick and other high performing leaders, they see all arrows pointing in a common direction and aligned with the overall district goal. When I present on this topic, I show three pictures (Figure 13). The first picture has little arrows pointing in different directions. The second picture shows one big arrow with smaller arrows pointing in different directions inside the big arrow. The third picture shows one big arrow with all small arrows within pointing forward in alignment. All arrows are pointing in a common direction – that's what the scorecard process helps us do.

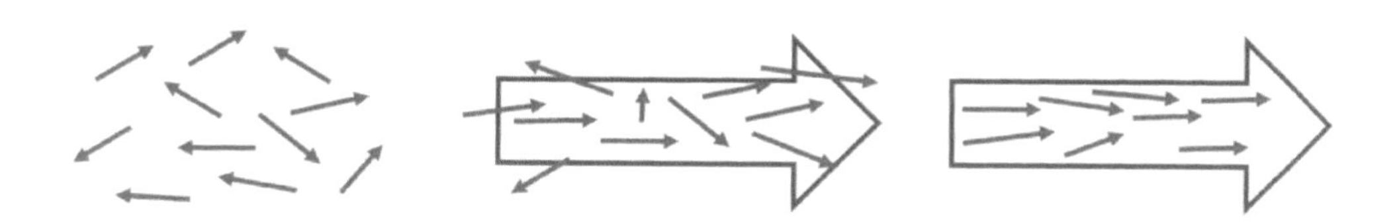

*Figure 13. Alignment of the Organization*

The big arrow represents the strategic plan and direction of the organization. The small arrows represent the alignment of departments and schools to the overall organization. All arrows lined up represent good strategic goals and aligned execution, like Rick and his team demonstrated.

We've been in work environments where arrows are all over the place. Work feels chaotic and reactive. The work is not connected to a strategic direction (defined by the big arrow). No alignment across the organization exists. The likelihood of achieving positive results diminishes. Even if we happen to hit the mark in one year, we may fail to sustain results over time.

Our overall goal is to align schools and departments to achieve positive results. That doesn't mean everyone's doing the same thing. Some strategic actions are hardwired across the organization. Varied actions occur within schools and departments while still aligning to the overall goals. Developing school and department scorecards that include results measures, progress measures, and strategic actions help us stay aligned.

## Short Cycle Improvement Process

Once we cascade the scorecard process to schools and departments, we begin a short cycle, or more frequent check ins, improvement process. Applying a continuous improvement process is expected of all leaders. There are certain actions that we want to standardize across leaders in the organization.

- Develop a school/department scorecard that indicates results measures, progress measures and strategic actions that align to the organizational scorecard.
- Apply a short-cycle improvement process from every 45 to 75 days in every school and department.
- School and department leaders share areas working well and those needing improvements with their leaders, teachers and staff, and families. This information will be shared differently with

the varying audiences. It's important to share information that reinforces the improvement work.

Every day counts when we are responsible for student learning and success. We need a process for reviewing results and evidence of our progress along the way. At a system level, leaders are looking at aggregate results. They can dig deeper into the meaning of aggregated results by reviewing data for schools and departments. The organizational scorecard drives the overall expectations for results. The data from the short-cycle improvement process sheds light on where things are working and where performance gaps are occurring earlier than an annual review. The point I'm trying to make here is that if you rely on data that takes longer to produce results, then you don't know what's happening, and you may miss an opportunity to make changes along the way that will produce better results.

Here are the steps for the short-cycle improvement process.

- Define the 45 to 75 progress goals driven by the school and department scorecards.
- Align core strategic actions with the measures and ensure everyone is trained and has a clear understanding of their expectations.
- With teams, review the progress measures every week or so to track progress. Talk about why the results are occurring and determine where the team needs to dig deeper into the data.
- Continue this process until the end of the cycle. Pull teams together to review progress toward the short cycle measurable goals. Focus on celebrating the bright spots, identifying the performance gaps and why they are occurring. Make assertations aligned

to the data rather than simply providing opinions. For some problems we can move toward a quick solution. For other problems, we need to apply a more in-depth improvement process to understand the real problem, determine the best result, and study the solution before putting it into practice.

We apply a short cycle improvement process for all pillars on the scorecard. Most schools and departments have goals aligned to people, service, and safety. In the academic areas, we include goals associated with student success. For nonacademic departments, most of the goals focus on operations and service. Regardless of the type of goals we have, we apply a short cycle improvement process to engage our teams in conversations about the data frequently. Remember, focusing on a small number of measurable goals by pillar increases our opportunities to succeed.

This process may seem overwhelming at first. Start small with your early adopters. Then cascade to other schools and departments over time. The early adopters will be eager to kick start designing their scorecards and using them to engage in conversations with their teams to inform the 45- to 75- day reviews. This gives you time to continue to develop all leaders to align behaviors to goals and values.

## Improvement Tools Used to Monitor Progress

We've reviewed how to apply a scorecard process (results measures, progress measures, and key actions) and a short cycle improvement process. As we are applying an improvement process, we can use some key tools to collect information and monitor progress with our teams. There are many improvement tools to draw from. I turn to two basic, yet powerful improvement tools – Stoplight Reports and Plus/Delta.

In many instances, we need tools to help us analyze what's working and what's not. The goal is to use these tools when we need to spend the right amount of time reflecting on our actions. We want to keep our approach simple without overcomplicating how we make improvements. A bad performance or outcome may be evident. In some instances, we need to understand why this is occurring. Process improvement tools help us see more clearly and deeply into issues causing problems. At other times, we may need to simply make a quick change to continue forward movement. This type of decision reminds me of a childhood story. I was early elementary age. My yard was the arena for football, basketball, and baseball games. One day, I asked my dad to join me on an imaginary baseball field in our backyard. To start the game, we stood beside each other in the yard. Under my direction we began singing the National Anthem. Hearing the unpleasant sound of our voices, I tugged on his shirt suggesting that we make a quick adjustment and simply say the Pledge of Allegiance. That was an easy decision that had a quick, agreeable solution.

Many barriers we face do not have quick solutions, yet they are not extremely complicated to solve. That's where tools like a Stoplight Report and a Plus/Delta come in handy.

*Stoplight Reports*

To stay organized and avoid dropping the ball on executing our core strategic actions, we recommend using a stoplight report. It is a versatile tool that can be used in many ways. A stoplight report is a tracking and communication tool.

It helps us track progress, share information up and down the organization, and keep the priorities in front of everyone.

You may recall how we used a stoplight report to capture rounding information from rounding with employees and customers. Leaders who use this tool demonstrate that they value peoples' opinions. When we use a stoplight report to capture rounding information, we track information, monitor progress, and transparently communicate with our teams.

- Green items are things that have been addressed and are complete.
- Yellow items are things in progress.
- Red items are things that cannot be done along with an explanation of why they can't be done.

We can also use a stoplight report to track progress on our short cycle improvements. This green-yellow-red breakdown is incredibly useful to track the status of what's working, where we are making progress, and where we are falling short. The stoplight report keeps everyone informed about the team's progress on the most important priorities. We use evidence to guide us on how we code progress using green, yellow, or red. At the beginning, middle and end of the 45- to 75- day cycle, everyone has a clear understanding of the priorities and progress made. If the stoplight report reveals that there isn't enough movement in the right direction, we make needed adjustments going into the next cycle.

Let's review an example of one measure to track and how to record it in a stoplight report. Let's say at a school, we have an 85% attendance goal. School attendance has proven to be a good lead or predictive measure of student success. Teachers track this goal every day. At the end of the week, a school leader compiles the information in a stoplight report. A core team at the school reviews the stoplight report that includes weekly results by class. This core team also reviews overall attendance for each student by class to put a face on the data. They can see which students are on target with the goal (green), students that are close to achieving the attendance goal (yellow), and students who are falling well short of the attendance goal (red).

The school collects this data and at the end of 45 days, compiles the information to share with teachers at their data meetings. The conversations with teachers focus on where they are succeeding and why, where they are making progress and why, and where they are falling behind and why. Two outcomes occur from these meetings. First, teachers who have a high attendance rate can talk about the strategies they are using that others can learn from and adopt. Second, the review of data over 45 days guides teachers and additional support staff on where they need to offer interventions to students and families to get students to school and keep them there.

Here's another example that describes how our Studer Education team applies a short cycle improvement process to monitor progress on important goals associated with the TeacherReady program referenced earlier in the book. For TeacherReady, our alternative teacher certification program, we use a stoplight report to track the time it takes students to complete each of 12 lessons. The program gives students an opportunity to work at their own pace. We've discovered the time it takes for students to complete each lesson contributes to students having the best opportunity to successfully complete the program. We've developed our instructional and advising model to align to this recommended pace. We code students' progression using green, yellow and red codes. Green means students are aligned with the recommended pace; yellow means they are tracking one to two weeks behind; and red means they are tracking more than two weeks behind.

Advisors are assigned specific students and stay with those students throughout the program (for about a year). At weekly team meetings, the aggregate data are reviewed for each code. The overall goal is 80% of the students are progressing on time. Each week the team engages in a conversation about what's working and why and where challenges exist and why. The bigger challenges shift into an intensive review process to clearly identify the problem, the root cause of the problem and possible solutions. The team applies a possible solution. They pay close attention to how the solution works. Also, both the advisors and the lesson instructors know the students who are progressing on time (green), falling slightly behind (yellow); and falling way behind (red). Reviewing each student's weekly progress directs advisors and instructors on their next week's priorities to support students.

Using the stoplight report as a tracking and communication tool while applying a short cycle improvement process is powerful. People engage in conversations about ways to improve. The process gives teams a way to review data, engage in meaningful conversations, and make improvement decisions.

*Plus/Delta*

Plus/Delta is a quality tool that provides a simple method for individuals or teams to reflect and engage in improvement conversations. The Plus/Delta tool can help inform us of the changes needed to achieve higher levels of performance.

We talk about the pluses by asking people to identify the things that are working and explain why. These are the items that we want to keep doing or do more of. It's also important to identify the opportunities for improvement or challenges we are facing. These are the things to change so that the individuals or teams can be more effective. Our goal is to record deltas that are specific and action oriented. We engage in meaningful conversations centered on evidence to determine where to improve. As indicated in the stoplight example, each week a team of teachers reviews aggregate data and individual student data on school attendance. The team then uses a Plus/Delta tool to talk about the data, asking what's working and what supporting evidence exists. The evidence also indicates where we have challenges.

As you can see, we can apply a Plus/Delta tool to almost anything we do. It's a great way to do a formative check on current, real-time approaches to achieving goals. It can be used in straightforward ways. For example, we can use a Plus/Delta tool to assess the value of a meeting. We can use a weekly Plus/Delta with our teams to talk about how well we completed our priorities for the week. We can use the tool with students. Ask what worked well with today's lesson and why? Where did you face challenges with today's lesson and why? When we make changes in our processes, we can apply a plus/delta. What worked well with the new process and why? What challenges did you face and why?

The Plus/Delta tool provides tremendous benefits. It enables us to engage our teams in meaningful improvement conversations. It gives us information we can act on quickly. It also gives people on our teams a chance to give input. Applying a Plus/Delta tool is a non-threatening way to gain insight. Here are ground rules for using the tool.

1. All opinions are heard.
2. Listen without being defensive.

3. Ask for team members to provide specific feedback.
4. Use the information – some information triggers immediate actions; other information may need more study.

The Plus/Delta tool helps us reflect, gain input, and act. Our actions are thoughtful, focused, and collaborative.

Here's a creative way to help us personally improve. This approach reinforces Principle 6 Be Accountable. Use the tool to reflect on your work at the end of a week. Ask, what's worked well for me this week? Where could I improve? For some areas, there may be something small we can change that will make a big difference. Link that one action to your personal growth goals. And stay with it to sustain the changed behavior.

The Plus/Delta tool is versatile and efficient. It provides a productive way to engage our teams in meaningful conversations about the bright spots and areas needing improvements.

## Leaders Feeling Empowered to Act

Aligning behaviors with goals and values is where the rubber meets the road in becoming an excellent organization. Typically, leaders are good at developing a strategic plan. However, they have sometimes fallen short of executing the plan to achieve and sustain high performing results at the department and school levels.

The strategic plan builds the "fence" for the organization. Organizational leaders have the freedom within the fence to make decisions and act. To do so, they need clear direction. Failing to put a system in place that aligns behaviors to goals and values leaves leaders guessing about where they have the authority to make decisions. When they guess wrong and receive negative feedback, they shy away from making other decisions. The organizational leaders then rely on where they feel safe, which is making independent decisions in their departments or schools.

Senior leaders get frustrated when leaders are "doing their own thing" in their departments and schools. They are also frustrated that organizational leaders depend on them for direction before making decisions. They wonder why leaders aren't being more proactive. Senior leaders have asked me this question – *"Why can't leaders take ownership and make their own decisions rather than coming to me for direction?"*

Organizational leaders need to understand the degree of autonomy they have within the "fence." It's senior leadership's responsibility to make that clear. To support organizational leaders to feel empowered to make independent decisions, senior leaders need to focus on these five actions.

**First, senior leaders need to make sure organizational leaders have the necessary skills to apply a continuous improvement process outlined in this chapter.** Organizational leaders are expected to involve employees in conversations on cascading the goals to their units and determining actions and measures of success. This process provides the groundwork for organizational leaders to facilitate short cycle improvement conversations and to check how their teams are progressing toward the outcomes every 45 to 75 days.

**Second, senior leaders help organizational leaders understand where they can make decisions.** If there are places where they should not make decisions, senior leaders need to let them know that. Most leaders want to do the right thing. They can't read senior leaders' minds. If senior leaders know where the boundaries are, they need to tell them. If not, the boundaries are being defined, leaving room for coaching organizational leaders along the way. Both are acceptable approaches. What's not acceptable is holding people accountable to ever evolving expectations that organizational leaders don't understand. Once the boundaries are defined, senior leaders can hold them to tighter expectations.

**Third, senior leaders encourage leaders to create ideas or solutions before bringing a problem to them**. Senior leaders let organizational leaders know that they can come to them with questions as they are trying to solve a problem. As organizational leaders advance their skills, they will reduce their dependency. When organizational leaders ask a question, senior leaders can turn the question back to them by asking, what would you do? If the organizational leader says, I don't know. Then senior leaders ask if you knew what would you do? Asking a question back to the questioner provides a great opportunity for "coaching in the moment."

**Fourth, from time to time, senior leaders round with leaders, asking how they are doing and where they need help.** I find that our high performers may not come for help when they could really benefit from senior leaders' guidance. High performers believe they should handle things on their own. As senior leaders, we want high performers to come to us for assistance. Also, **all** organizational leaders need meaningful touch points with their senior leaders.

**Fifth, senior leaders recognize organizational leaders when they see them being proactive with actions and doing it well.** Senior leaders provide specific feedback about what organizational leaders have accomplished. It's positive for the organizational leader, and it also teaches others what good practices look like. Using recognition promotes teachable moments.

I've found when senior leaders apply these five actions, most organizational leaders grow to become empowered leaders, assuming they have solid leadership skills to draw from. One of the best feelings I experience as an executive leader occurs when leaders on our team gain confidence to lead their teams and do it well. They depend on themselves more and on me less.

## Chapter 7 Summary

Aligning behaviors with goals and values requires leaders to advance their skills to manage a systematic approach to achieving results in every school and department. The culminating results impact the overall organizational results.

Every leader leads a 45- to 75- day short cycle improvement process. The focus is on executing key actions while continuously assessing progress using good predictors of success. The organizational leaders apply scorecards and short cycle improvement processes to execute the strategic direction of the organization. This alignment reinforces consistency of leadership practices with aligned behaviors to achieve high performing results.

The El Dorado County Office of Education (EDCOE) provides an excellent example of Principle 7. Dr. Ed Manansala, an executive leader, is the County Superintendent of Schools for EDCOE. Working with one of our coaches, Dr. Pat Greco, Dr. Manansala and the Human Resources team tackled an urgent problem in record time. EDCOE had 785 students on a waitlist for afterschool care because the county had inadequate staffing for their extended day after school care program. Parents were unable to find options for before or after-school care, which was disrupting families from being able to manage their lives and ensure their children were in a safe place.

The HR team set a goal to reduce the number of unfilled positions in the hard to fill areas to reduce the student waitlist. HR team members focused on cross-collaborative input and feedback across teams to get the insights from those closest to the issue. They received ideas to apply to achieve the goal. They broke the barriers of old practices with new ideas.

The EDCOE team deployed a short cycle improvement approach over 5 weeks to solve this problem. The team

- clarified the measures they would track on a weekly basis (dashboard).
- reported dashboard measures and progress to the executive cabinet every week.
- worked directly with the Extended Day Program Manager and her team members in extended day care through weekly huddles to review data and create a “safe” space for the team to test ideas.
- continued to track data on ideas, weeding out those that were not working and continuing to apply those that worked.

In five weeks of intense short cycles of improvements in weekly huddles, the EDCOE team removed all 785 students from the waitlist. This departmental goal aligned to a key EDCOE goal for providing great customer service to their respective El Dorado region. The HR department applied specific actions to help the broader organization achieve its goals and values. What an accomplishment by the EDCOE Human Resources team and the senior leaders! They did so by leveraging ideas of the team members closest to the work to get to workable solutions. The weekly data and team huddles drove conversations that led to aligning specific actions to achieve a challenging goal in record time.

EDCOE connected the Elephant and the Rider to travel a path that led to solving a problem that made a difference in the lives of students and their families. Dr. Manansala leads his team to apply many of the tactics outlined in this book. EDCOE has adopted their Standards of Excellence to lay the groundwork for defining their culture. The leaders round with their teams, facilitate weekly huddles, use a scorecard to define the measures that matter, apply the Plus/Delta and Stoplight Report tools to monitor and communicate progress, and engage teams in short cycle improvement meetings to align team goals, identify cross team barriers, and engage the people closest to the work in solving problems and addressing barriers that support students and their families. EDCOE provides a great example for creating aligned and consistent leadership practices that produce positive results.

# 8

# COMMUNICATE AT ALL LEVELS

*People know what they do matters.*

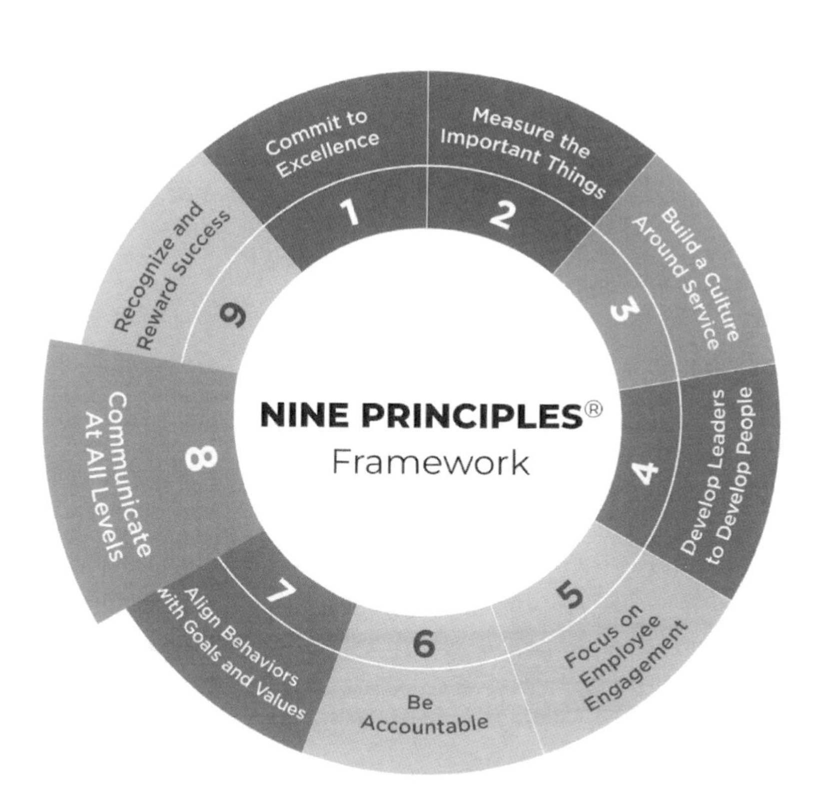

Principle 8 Communicate at All Levels is fundamental to achieving individual and organizational excellence. It's important enough to be a unique principle, and it's part of the other eight. Applying the principles to hardwire excellence depends on how well we communicate at all levels. When we fail to communicate in ways that people understand, we lose momentum. When our partners receive their initial results on surveys it seems the communication items tend to receive low scores. Let's focus on how we can shift communication from a weakness to a strength.

In the first chapter of this book, I summarized one form of negative communication that factors into poor communication and stops the organizational flywheel from spinning – We/They messages. It's when someone positions themselves in a positive light at the expense of someone else. Doing so, we fail to live our organizational values. We must simply stop communicating with We/They messages. That's essential to strengthening communication.

We have personal values, and we lead organizations with values that define how we treat others. These two closely align. Communicating effectively is first and foremost about living our values. Here's how we do that.

1. Reflect on our personal values. Reconnect personal values to organizational values.
2. Start every day remembering that our actions will be guided by these values.
3. Ensure that we align our actions to our values, even in the most difficult times.
4. Stay true to our values by not letting anyone or any circumstance get in the way of our living these values.

The connection to our personal and organizational values influences the way we communicate with others. When we know what we stand for, it's easier to use our values to guide the way we engage and interact with others. Also, if we feel like we are getting off track, we can always connect to our values and then re-group.

We can be our own worst enemy without intending to be. For example, think about times when we are putting together a presentation to share. We have 15 minutes and 40 slides! Who is the presentation most important to – us or the audience? Us – it's more about what we want to say than about communicating what's most beneficial to the audience. Our actions are not malicious. We just don't take the right amount of time to consider what others need to hear that is most helpful to them. As experts in certain areas, we have a lot to share. The key to communicating effectively is determining what to share, how to share information, and what not to share. Most of the time less is more, meaning we offer focused information to people to process more deeply.

## Purpose of Our Communication

The best communication occurs when we respect, inspire, and encourage others to be and do their best. Over the years I've learned that people tend to rate communication higher when people know how what they do contributes to the organization. We seldom think deeply enough before crafting messages to people. Effectively communicating is a key leadership skill that doesn't come naturally. We need to develop that skill to be good leaders.

We communicate all day, every day. We communicate in different ways, in different places, and for many reasons. In any communication, we have outcomes we are trying to achieve. We may want to communicate things that are happening, bright spots and wins we can celebrate as a team, important dates coming up, or any number of other things. We communicate in the halls, on the phone, by email or reports, and the list goes on. Leaders do this naturally, but to do it effectively, we need to consider what is important for people to know. That is, what is the purpose for communicating? What are we communicating? Why are we communicating a particular message?

The purpose of our communication is to help us focus on what we want to communicate and how we communicate. For example, the point of communication may be to share information, problem solve, analyze a situation, or change behavior. It may be a call to action. Regardless of the reason, our messages focus on a purpose we hope to achieve. We want our purpose to be clear to others.

Our purpose for communicating something drives the way we communicate with others. We start by determining why we are communicating a message, what we need to communicate to achieve the purpose, and how we will communicate to deliver the best message to get a positive outcome.

What gets in the way of communicating with purpose? At Studer Education, one of our Standards of Excellence is

"Make the complex simple." Working to apply this standard with our team, I was drawn to Lisa Bodell's book, *Why Simple Wins*. We get trapped spending our days in mundane tasks. We have too many meetings and emails that seem to get in the way of accomplishing our work. Or, we have broken processes that require layers of time we didn't plan on. Our goal is to spend time on the work we value and things that matter.

The principles leading up to this point focused on tactics that make the complex simple. That doesn't mean they are simple to do. Rather, we work to simplify how we apply them.

Bodell claims that something is properly simplified when it is

- minimal as possible or there are just enough steps to get something done, but not too many.
- understandable as possible or things are defined in clear, straightforward language.
- repeatable as possible or things are easy for people to do over and again.
- accessible as possible or simple things are made available and visible.

Recently, I was in a meeting to learn about some new policies that had been implemented across the states. I was sitting at a table with a group. When the session was over, we started talking about the message. Here's how the conversation went. See if this sounds familiar. Someone at our table said, "*What did she say? I couldn't follow the information provided. I was trying to read the slides and listen at the same time. The print was so tiny, I gave up and just listened. There were a lot of slides with a lot of information. I hope we have access to the slides. We came here to learn about the new policies we are required to put in place. Did you all understand what we are supposed to do?"* This example violates Bodell's recommendations. I keep these four recommendations in front of me to check my communication messages. I hope they help you as well.

If we are not clear with our message like the example, we may blame people for failing to act. People sending the message may say something like this. *"They didn't understand because they weren't listening. How many times do we have to explain this?"* Poor communication adds unnecessary frustrations to our work. Let's look at some ways we can be good communicators.

## Why Starting with the Why Matters

Importantly, communication is about reinforcing purpose in our work. Communicating well means considering why we are communicating. Having the right attitude and approach behind the communication message influences the way people perceive and respond to our message.

Before we communicate, first ask, why should anyone care about what I am saying? People care when they see that the message has a direct relationship to how they feel and what they are experiencing. It's less about what we want to say and more about what we decide to say to help others manage their work in meaningful ways.

How do we structure messages to get the right information to the right people at the right time and in the right way? We suggest using what we call the "why, what, how" approach. "Why" focuses on communicating to the audience why the message is important to them. "What" focuses on what is happening or what we are communicating. "How" focuses on how things will work or what we need to do.

The why, what, how approach isn't always our natural way of communicating. We tend to move right to what and how. When we do, our teams may act on a request without ever knowing why in the world they are doing a specific action.

We often have a message to communicate, and we, understandably, go straight to the "what." That is, we start with *what* we want to communicate. When we begin with the "what," team members don't know why and how the message being shared relates to them. We may even lose them before we ever get to the "why," if we get there at all. Our research shows, that the "why" is the best place to start a message. Helping people see the "why" allows us to connect people with the information and why it is meaningful to them. The "why" helps us gain buy-in and builds a collaborative spirit. We start with connecting to why the message is important to others.

Sharing the "why" in a message is so important. When we say, "share the why," whose why are we talking about? We aren't talking about **our** why. We are talking about the **audience's** "why." The message is for and to them, so they need to know how that message connects with them. This means that when we define the "why," the words we choose are related to our team's "why." We explain why the message is important, why it relates to them, and how the message being communicated affects them.

I was talking with an executive leader. For two years, he focused on communicating starting with why. One day he said, *"I always start with why, but I don't feel like people are responding. I'm not seeing different behaviors."* I asked, *"Whose why are you starting with?"* He said, *"My why."* I said, *"Oh, I see. Consider starting with the "why" for the people you're communicating with. People are less interested in why something is important to you and more interested in how that message relates to them."* Good communication occurs when we think about the audiences "why" and craft our communication to meet their needs rather than our own.

Some of our most powerful communication occurs when we are calling people to action or calling for a change in behavior. Sharing the why in this type of communication is particularly important. Specifically, getting to the heart of the team's "why" is crucial in a call to action. What seems like a good behavior change or call to action to us may not seem great to our teams unless we make connections for them on why the change is important. To change people's behavior, tell them what's in it for them. That is, tell them how the change helps them, their team, and the organization. People want to know how the change affects them and their work. Make this connection for people. They will respond more positively and readily.

To know how to connect with our team's why, we need to know our team. Then it's much easier to share a meaningful why. Our communication is more genuine because we've developed good relationships with them. Sharing the why also allows us to move beyond just informing to reassuring and affirming our teams. Starting with the why shows we care, which leads to building trust.

It's important to note that different groups may have different whys even if we have the same purpose for a message. It's important to tailor the why to each audience.

Once we capture the why in the message, we can craft the what and how. These three components together help us ensure the messages we share are focused on our purpose, written using clear and intentional language, shared in brief and concise ways, and appeal to the rational and emotional sides of our audience. It takes time to craft this kind of message, but it's time well worth spending.

## Helpful Communication Tips

Using key words in our messages is important. It's also important to think about how we interact with others. The way we engage with people and the words we choose influence how people perceive our level of communication. There's so much to being a good communicator. In this section, I provide several short tips on how to be a better communicator.

- **Craft a message considering how the words will make someone feel**. We appeal to both the rational side of people and the emotional side of people. If we fail to consider the emotional side of the message or what emotions the message might evoke, we may fail to meet the intended outcomes simply because our message wasn't crafted well. It's important to consider what we want people to know *and* feel when we share our message.
- **Think more, write less. Mark Twain once wrote, "I didn't have time to write you a short letter, so I wrote you a long one."** Mark Twain's ironic quote perfectly captures the idea of think more, write less. The best messages are brief and intentional. Also, we are more successful at communicating when we spend time where it matters most. Take time to prepare and plan the message.

  Good communication occurs when we spend more time crafting and planning a message and less time talking. This isn't always easy, and it may be a shift in mindset. We seldom if ever place "crafting a message" on our calendars like we do scheduling meetings. This added time saves time and heartache in the long run. Our messages become shorter, more concise, and clear. They are connected to why this message is important to hear.

It's easy to begin crafting a message and get lost in the details. We want to share lots of information to keep our teams informed. The question, though, is do they need all that information? In our experiences working with leaders, we've found that less is more. It's best to focus on what the audience needs to know rather than what we want to say. Remember, keep it simple. Spend time getting to the heart of the message and keep that focus.

- **Pay ridiculous attention to people**. Listen intently to what they are saying, ask probing questions to learn more, act where needed, and follow-up to close the loop. Look in their eyes and move computers and phones aside. At our quarterly strategy sessions, I have one rule. Put computers and mobile phones away and take notes using pen and paper. Why? Our entire team comes together in person several times a year. Our job is to pay ridiculous attention to each other.
  - Give the person speaking our full attention.
  - Actively listen, jotting down questions to make sure we understand.
  - Focus on understanding what people are saying rather than thinking about what we want to say.
  - Summarize and confirm what we think we heard.
- **Turn someone's question back to them to answer**. Someone comes to you with a question that you would like for them to think more about rather than providing the answer. Turn the question back to them. If they say they don't know, ask them what they would do if they did know. Nine times out of ten the person will share their thoughts.

- **Connect actions or changes back to input received.** People want to know that their input matters. That doesn't mean that people always get their way. They want to know why decisions were made. Therefore, connect decisions back to the input provided and how that information played into a decision.

  As we described, we receive input from people on the survey results. Here's an example of how we connect our communication back to the input. A leader may say to the team, *"You may recall that when we rolled out the survey results, you recommended having one-on-one meetings with me. I appreciate your feedback and specific suggestions. After hearing the feedback, I will start to schedule 30- minute monthly meetings with each of you. We will continue working on a common agenda for those meetings to make sure we use our time wisely."*
- **Challenge generalizations**. We hear people make statements like, They believe... Everyone feels... Our instinct is to react to these statements with a response. Instead, ask who are "they?" When you refer to "everyone," who are you referring to? Getting more unambiguous information helps the person be more specific with identifying where the problem is occurring. Also, it's important for people to stop using generalized statements to communicate.
- **Don't feel pressured to answer a tough question right away**. Make sure you know the question being asked. Express that you want to provide the best answer and need some time to gather information that will help you do that. Let people know when you will get back with them, how it will be communicated, and follow-up with an answer.
- **Personalize messages and invitations with the word, "you."** Writing a message that is authentic

and includes the word "you" let's people know that they are the most important part of the message. At times we intend to make personal connections with our messages. Including the word "you" throughout the message helps us do just that. When I invited Dr. KK Owen to round with me here's the message I sent to her,

*Hello KK,*

*I hope you are doing well and your connection with your partners is off to a good start. I know you are excited to see them after a year of zoom connections. You are important to our coaching team by serving as a leader to so many of your colleagues. As the coaching team gets back on the road, I want to ensure that you and your colleagues have what you need to do the important work you do. It's important for me to learn from you.*

*I am scheduling a rounding session with our coaches to gain insight into your needs and to learn more about what your partner organizations are facing. Thank you for agreeing to schedule a rounding session with me on August 27th at 9:00 a.m. I look forward to our time together.*

*Thank you for taking 20 minutes of your time to connect with me.*

*Janet*

- **Help employees carry their own messages**. Have you ever heard someone carry a message like this to a leader? Notice how the leader responds by reverting the responsibility of the message back to the employee.

Employee: *"I'm here representing our team. The deadline for the completion of the project was unreasonable. That's why we didn't achieve the goal."*

Leader: *"Is that what you believe?"*

Employee: *"No, that's not my individual opinion. I am here for the team."*

Leader: *"I want to hear what you believe. If others have an opinion, I need to hear that directly from them. What do you think occurred?"*

The leader puts the ball back in the court of this individual and team. People learn to stop carrying messages from others and become accountable for themselves.

- **Be as transparent as possible**. Consistently share relevant information to help people understand why actions are occurring, what is being done, and how we are moving forward. If there is information you can't share, tell them that. It's better to share what you can than to be evasive. Share both good and bad news. People want leaders to be honest. At times, leaders may not share information believing they are protecting employees from difficult news. Not communicating difficult news makes people feel anxious about their jobs.
- **Communicate clear, simple messages**. I can't over emphasize this enough. People respond better to simplicity as outlined in this chapter. Verify that people understand your message by asking them what they heard. Listen to their response ensuring the message is clear.
- **Regularly communicate wins and bright spots**. As we will focus on in the next chapter, wins are

occurring every day in education. Make this type of communication intentional and recognize at least one win or bright spot a day. When you do, you may find you want to recognize more. It makes people feel good about their work and reinforces why they choose to be in the education profession.

## Helpful Communication Tools

I close the chapter with what I consider three simple, yet powerful communication tools. First, we can structure our meeting agendas to include ways to communicate wins and cascade important information to the organization. Team huddles give us a way to do short, quick touchpoints to reinforce that we are working on the right things and addressing immediate barriers. The 3-2-1 tool provides a simple tool that communicates how we are tracking the most important work.

*Make Communication Part of Your Meeting Agendas*

We don't hear too many people say they love meetings. Meetings are supposed to be an engine of collaboration, problem-solving and improvement. The purpose of meetings is to tap into the energy and expertise of a team. We want our meetings to matter to our teams by providing good structure that promotes positive engagement. I suggest that when structuring meetings, we spend at least 70% of the time engaging in conversations about how to improve, solve problems, and move input to action. The other part of the meeting includes important announcements or information sharing.

We recommend that leaders start the meeting with a "connect to purpose" or recent wins. We can tell a story that reinforces why we do what we do. It can be a success story with aligned proven results. We can also spend the first 5 minutes talking about some key wins.

Much of the meeting may be spent assessing progress on our goals. We may include ongoing progress measures followed by a Plus/Delta approach asking what's working and why and what's challenging and why. We then focus on our next improvement actions. We could also focus the meeting on discussing a complex problem or a broken process that needs to be improved. The goal of the meeting is to use data and input to generate improvement discussions.

We end the meeting spending the last 5 to 10 minutes summarizing the most important items in the meeting that will be shared with others. The best way to cascade communication is to ensure that people in the organization get the same information around the same time. At the end of the meeting, we summarize what information needs to be cascaded, what the message is, and how it will occur. Employees get suspicious of leaders when some people hear things and others do not. Consistency of communication with important messages builds a more trusting workplace environment.

*Connect Often with Team Huddles*

A huddle is a short meeting meant to occur often so that a core team can be informed and aligned on the work that needs to be done. The purpose of the team huddle is to increase team productivity, accountability, and optimism. We don't solve difficult problems during huddles. Problem-solving occurs in another format using appropriate problem-solving tools. Rather, we touch base on key outcomes and actions that inform us to do the work that matters most.

Here are several suggestions for holding huddles.

- When conducting a daily huddle use technology or interactions that allow teams to see each other face-to-face. Also, record, take notes, and follow-up.
- Keep the huddle to no more than 20 to 30 minutes.
- Start with a positive and end with a positive. Spread opportunities for people to share positives.
- Schedule time for the leaders to provide important announcements if there are any that day. During the meeting, selected leaders will provide information on these three areas:
    - What's up in the next 24 hours or from the time you have one huddle to the next?
    - What are the results on daily metrics?
    - Where is your team getting stuck? Again, the purpose is not to solve problems with this group but to identify "getting stuck" areas. These areas may need the attention of the leader, or they could be pushed to a team to solve. Issues may be simple or complex. The follow-up action depends on the complexity of the problem.

Team huddles are particularly helpful when there's a sense of urgency to make changes. For example, I started using team huddles when our team shifted to a completely virtual environment during the COVID pandemic. We huddled for 20 minutes every day at the same time and followed the agenda above. Our team didn't miss a beat. We continued to achieve our goals and became highly connected with each other. We've now shifted to holding huddles with our project and priorities teams. The purpose is to meet often, focus on results, and course correct areas that present barriers to get things accomplished.

*Simplify by Using a 3-2-1 Communication Tool*

As teachers, we've used the 3-2-1 reflection tool in our classes. We ask students to jot down three things they learned, two connections or insights they discovered, and one question they still have. On our Studer Education team we adapted the formative assessment tool to inform us on what's working as we apply the improvement actions aligned to specific outcomes. We use this tool to communicate formative results to others. As we applied the tool, we then shared it with our partner organizations to use.

The 3-2-1 communication tool powerfully communicates three important pieces of information. This tool can be used each week. It takes little time to complete and share rich information. Here's how I like to apply the 3-2-1 communication tool.

- Area 3 records themes on areas working well.
- Area 2 records the most pressing areas we need to improve.
- Area 1 records action steps underway.

This approach is one of my favorite simple communication tools. Why? Because it focuses on important things in front of us each week. We can apply the tool to most anything we are doing. We can summarize rounding sessions for the week. We can use the tool to chart how well we completed our weekly tasks aligned to our key actions on our quarterly goals. We can track specific progress measures that inform how well we are doing on a defined project in a timely way. For example, in our food services department we may want to improve the number of high school students eating school lunches. The department has undergone menu changes accompanied by a marketing campaign for high school students and their families. At the end of each week, the department team charts the number of students paying for lunch. They also randomly send students an online survey asking how they like the new menu. Students can accumulate points by taking the survey to get a free lunch.

At the end of the week the team reviews the following information.

- % of students who ate lunch compared to the improvement goal
- % increase in students eating lunch week over week
- Mean for students recommending the lunch to others
- Rolling average by item week over week
- Narrative input on three questions – What do you like about the new menu? What do you dislike about the new menu? What changes would you make to the menu?

At a weekly meeting, the food services team reviews the data and places information in the 3-2-1 tool that might look something like this.

3:Weekly Taco Tuesday continues to show improvements in numbers and satisfaction. *(area that shows consistent week over week positive results)*

2:The overall mean and percentage of students eating lunches is shifting up and down week by week. *(showing inconsistencies week over week)*

1:Using the input received over the first month, a student group is analyzing the information and designing a prototype menu to inform the food services committee. *(action taken to get more consistent week over week results)*

To dig deeper into why the inconsistencies are occurring, the 3-2-1 tool can be used by the food services team to engage in a Plus/Delta conversation. They answer these questions: Where do we see more consistent results with the new menu and why? Where are there inconsistencies and why? What do we need to do next week based on what we learned this week?

Like the food services team, the 3-2-1 communication tool helps us celebrate the wins, track our progress, and determine weekly priorities. The tool focuses on the progress measures of an overall goal. It provides a way to capture concise and actionable input. And the tool guides us on the right work for the next week. That's a powerful way to stay focused on the goal and keep people engaged.

## Chapter 8 Summary

The tips, tools and tactics for Principle 8 Communicate at All Levels reinforces that people want to know what they do has meaning. People want to be part of solution building, problem-solving, and idea creation. They like to contribute to their teams by being and interacting with each other. Aligning our communication approaches to help people engage and contribute to the organization gives us a better chance for employees to see communication as a leadership strength.

Today, it's easy to turn to digital devices to connect with people or send quick messages. This kind of communication can occur with little thought. Over time we may start losing the human touch of communication. As leaders, we can't allow this to occur in our organizations. Regardless of the way we deliver messages, we must remember our goal is to help people know what they do matters.

On one of my travels, I was eating dinner in a restaurant and saw a young couple (high school age) at the same restaurant eating dinner. Both were on their mobile phones waiting for their dinner to be served. I kept watching and was hopeful they were tying up some last-minute items before having dinner together. But that wasn't the case. They continued to stare into their phones. They spent most of their dinner together on their phones. I kept looking back to see if they were talking to each other. Every time I looked at their dinner table they were interacting with their phones, not each other. When I mentioned this to one of my friends, she said – they're probably talking to each other on their phones at the table. That was even more disturbing to me.

Communication is as much about how we show care and concern for others as it is sending and receiving a message. We need to listen intently to each other, be thoughtful, and plan ahead as we deliver our messages. Words are the way we express our thoughts and feelings to each other. They can build an inspired workplace or tear people down.

Developing positive relationships at work and in life is a timeless necessity to be a good person. Connecting with others means we listen intently and choose our words carefully. We smile, we laugh, we cry, and we express gratitude for the opportunity to be in someone's presence. Life and work are not about me or about you. It's about us having a meaningful place to work and providing excellent service to others. We can't do that alone. We need each other. We have a better opportunity to communicate well when we live our organizational and personal values always thinking about how our words influence the way others feel.

Dr. Ryan Carpenter, the Superintendent of Estacada School District, Oregon, practices the tactics outlined in this chapter as well as any leader I've worked with. So much so that he was selected as a Superintendent to Watch by the National Public Relations Association. The award recognized his ability to engage with and inform the school community and to expand two-way communication and outreach efforts. Here are some examples of what Dr. Carpenter does to enhance communication.

- Produces weekly video messages to families and the community
- Offers digital town halls to keep everyone up to date on what's occurring in the district
- Administers employee, parent, and student surveys and rolls out the results
- Holds daily huddles with his executive team focusing attention on the right work to achieve positive results
- Uses a Stoplight report to track rounding information and to track progress measures on the scorecard

Communicating at all levels has made an important difference in the Estacada School District. Effective communication is a critical part of an improvement mindset that extends to the workplace and community.

Dr. Carpenter leads the Estacada School District to apply key tactics associated with all nine principles. Communicating at all levels so that people know what they do matters is key to the district's success. He shows us that all other principles are much more powerful when we get communication right. It is key to building long-lasting relationships with students, their families, and employees. All other principles require that we apply their associated tools and tactics with effective communication skills outlined in this chapter. Communication occurs in everything we do. That's why Dr. Carpenter places this principle at the forefront of the improvement work he leads in the Estacada School District.

# 9

# REWARD AND RECOGNIZE SUCCESS

*Value and appreciate people working together to get results.*

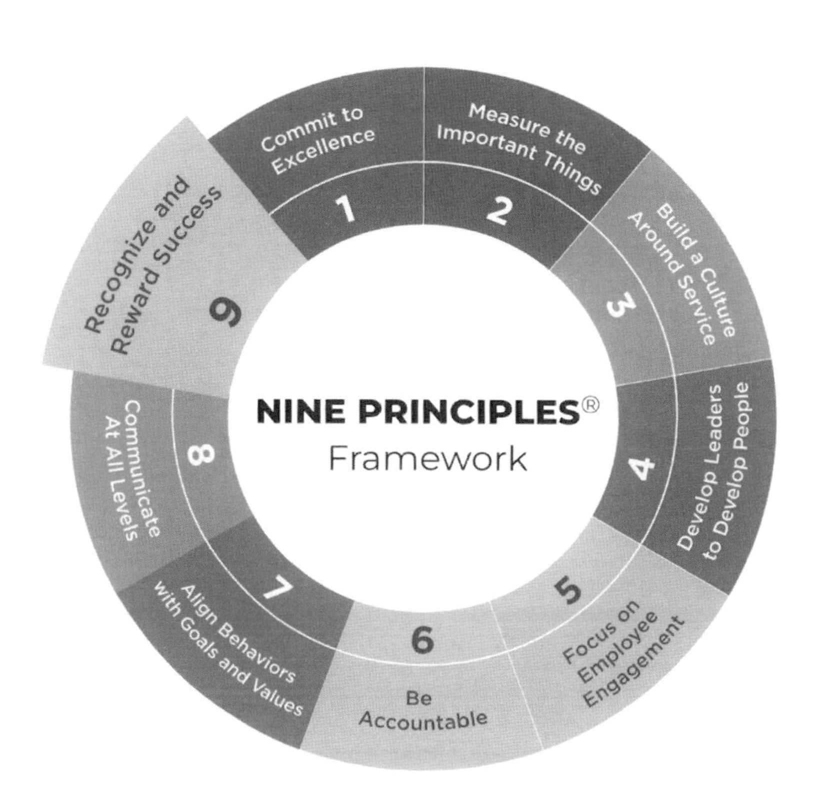

People want to be appreciated and recognized; it's part of human nature. There are many ways we can recognize people. We recognize people for good performance, and we appreciate people for the many types of contributions they make to our teams. We recognize people for living the organizational values, lending a helping hand to others, and doing meaningful work to give their best to students and their families.

When people are appreciated, they feel that people care about them as a person. When people get recognized and are appreciated, they have a better feeling about the organization, they know what they do matters, and they tend to be more satisfied at work.

To recognize people well, we need to know them – what they care about, what their goals are, and what makes them show up every day feeling good about their work. Also, we can learn from people exhibiting actions and behaviors that merit recognition. We've heard the phrase - *What gets recognized gets repeated.* Recognizing good performance helps people know what right behaviors and actions look like. Most people want to do a good job. When we recognize good work, we define expectations for our teams.

I've learned that we can't recognize the right actions and behaviors enough. I'm driven by goals and data. Recognizing people didn't naturally fit into what I did on the job. One of the lowest scored items on the first administration of the employee survey with my team was "recognizing people." When I shared the results, I asked our team why they felt this was an area to work on. I heard how the team valued being recognized for good performance and living our values. Leaving that meeting, I knew I needed to change my practices to include intentional ways of recognizing and appreciating people. I've made improvements over the years to make recognition a habit of practice. I continue to work on hardwiring Principle 9 Reward and Recognize Success. It's intentional work every day.

Developing our leadership skills to hardwire this principle is fundamental to being an excellent leader. It's not enough to occasionally reward and recognize people. We need to hardwire reward and recognition so that it happens often. It needs to be woven into the fabric of the culture.

Remember, we want to build an emotional bank account with our teams. It takes at least 3 interactions of positive feedback to 1 interaction of critical feedback to get people connected and engaged with our organization. This holds true for our interactions with students, their families, and employees. Most people we engage with want these positive interactions. This chapter is about recognizing and appreciating often.

Our goal is to be specific and genuine with our recognition. We've all experienced being in a room when we hear leaders say, *"Everybody's doing a great job." "All of you are responsible for the success."* It may be nice to hear, but it's an empty comment. Plus, people in the group who aren't doing a great job may think they are.

A better way to recognize people is to say something specific about what each person contributed. *"Mary – your approach to organizing the project and roles of the team contributed to the project meeting deadlines." "Jerry – your artistic ability put a unique touch on our new solution."* See the difference. The more specific we are, the more the person will appreciate the recognition. The more specific the compliment, the more meaningful it will be. The more specific the recognition, the more others know what attitudes, behaviors, or actions to emulate in order to receive recognition.

The need for recognition in education flows from the boardroom to the classroom. We expect board members to make supportive decisions and value what we do in our schools and departments. Yet, how often do we recognize them when they do? We expect employees to live our organizational values. Yet, how often do we recognize them when they do? We expect parents to be engaged in their child's education. Yet, how often do we recognize them when they do? We expect students to engage in their learning. Yet, how often do we recognize them when they do?

We are much more likely to provide critical feedback to people than to recognize the right behaviors often. Providing feedback to help board members, employees, parents, and students improve is important. We get better behaviors by giving more positives than negatives. Let's specifically recognize what people are doing right and do it often. Principle 9 is one of the most important in building healthy relationships with others. It is key to inspiring our teams to live the educational core values – purpose, worthwhile work, and making a difference.

# Managing Up

Managing up is positioning people and the organization well. It's a way for us to gain momentum to spin the flywheel. It's the opposite of positioning others in a negative light (we/they messages).

We manage up actions that are going well. It could be an achievement, improvement toward goals, and living the values. Managing up good work helps people know what is expected of them.

There are several ways to manage up. Manage up leaders, staff, yourself and your skill set, and your co-workers.

*Managing Up Leaders*

Managing up leaders positions the organization well, aligns desired behaviors, helps leaders be more visible, and creates opportunities for them to be recognized by others. Leaders do not get a lot of recognition. Managing up the things they do well helps them know how they are doing and what to do more of. I remember a time when an executive leader was transitioning into retirement and one of the leaders in the organization was hired to be the new executive leader. About 100 leaders in the organization wrote thank you notes to the executive retiring and the new executive coming into the position. They included one thing the individuals had done over the years that had a positive influence on them. At the broader transition meeting with the organization, the transitioning leader had an opportunity to share what he learned from the notes and what the notes meant to him. The retiring executive left the organization feeling like she made a meaningful contribution.

Leaders also appreciate people managing up others. Senior leaders don't know all the good work that people are doing across the organization. Many of the superintendents we work with take time to visit schools and departments. Wouldn't it be nice if principals and department leaders sent 2 or 3 manage ups to the superintendent so that when she made the visit, she could show appreciation to the individuals in very specific ways. The person receiving appreciation tells others in the organization and suddenly, the superintendent is perceived as being more visible.

When we hold our conferences, we review with each other who is attending. Our team provides me with an overview of who the leaders are and what they do well. It gives me a chance to make a meaningful personal connection with leaders. I enjoy learning about people we work with. It gives me purpose and makes my work worthwhile.

*Manage Up Employees and Staff*

As leaders, let's make managing up employees to others a priority. Collect the accomplishments and improvements of employees and staff and share them with leaders.

Let's say that our facilities department worked around the clock 48 hours before the school year began to get the new school ready to open on the first day of school. The contractor fell behind schedule with the completion of the work, pushing the facilities department to a tighter timeline to do their part. Rather than disrupt the start of school for teachers, students and their families, a core team of facilities employees did the work necessary to open school on time. The principal sent a note to the superintendent, teachers and staff at the school recognizing the facilities department by describing what their team did to open the school on time. The superintendent connected with each person on the facilities team thanking them in specific ways. The school hosted an afterschool appreciation event to recognize the team. The accomplishment was highlighted in the monthly newsletter sent to faculty, staff, and families. How do you think the facilities team felt? Do you think they are motivated to continue that level of service? The facilities team felt appreciated and will continue to provide the highest level of service. They know how their work contributed to teachers, students, and families.

*Manage Up Yourself and Your Coworkers*

When we manage up team members, they feel better about themselves and what they contribute. It also makes those receiving services feel confident in the person providing that service.

Families feel lucky when their child gets a teacher who shows care and concern for their child and provides a learning environment where their child can be successful. At the end of the year, families are apprehensive about their child having a new teacher. What if this occurred? The child's teacher wrote a short note to each child's family, managing up the skill set of their new teacher. The new teacher wrote a note to each child's family introducing who they are and their skill set. How would that family feel? Like they got lucky once again.

I've provided several ways to manage up other people. The purposes of managing up are to

- reduce people's anxiety when changes are occurring.
- show people what doing the right thing looks like.
- appreciate the contributions of people who make a difference in the lives of students and their families.

Recognition is a necessary practice to hardwire in our organizations. When we do, we start to see a positive shift in our culture.

## Ways to Reward and Recognize People

Rewards take on a broad meaning. Rewards include promotions, pay increases, new opportunities, and recognition. People see rewards given authentically if the rewards work together and reinforce each other.

We continue to hear the need to align teachers and staff salaries to be more competitive in the market. People also want opportunities to advance their skills or positions. Recognizing and appreciating people does not take the place of providing better pay and opportunities for promotion. On the other hand, pay and promotion alone will not retain people in the workforce. Similarly, giving employees annual awards provides a systematic approach to recognizing people. Complementing that with specific, consistent, frequent, and authentic recognition builds a culture focused on recognizing good performance and behaviors.

Everyone in the organization is involved in recognizing others. Leaders recognize employees. Employees recognize each other. Leaders, teachers, and staff recognize students and their families. As an added benefit, making recognition part of our work inspires students and their families to return the recognition.

The good news is that we have complete control over the way we recognize and appreciate others. There are no budget limitations to expressing care and concern for employees and recognizing them for their contributions.

Recognition is so important; we want to make it a habit of practice in the workplace. We know people want to be recognized differently. One of our first actions may be to create a process for asking people how they prefer to be recognized and then honor it, giving people an opportunity to change their mind and update their preferences. I've found that we build trust as we systematically recognize people in sincere ways. With growing trust, people feel more comfortable being recognized.

At some point, I get this question? What if people are recognizing people who shouldn't be? First, we need to train people in what good recognition looks like. The goal is not to create a place where people are haphazardly recognizing others. Rather, we want to be specific about what we are recognizing people for. We want to integrate recognition and appreciation in our culture that is timely, specific, and accurate. Second, we want to attend to how low performers are being recognized. They tend to be good at making up for their bad behavior by turning around and doing something helpful. Leaders or peers may fall into their trap. Low performers are counting on us sending mixed messages. I've seen leaders feel compelled to give someone a compliment after they've addressed a negative behavior head on. Why? Because most of us want to be liked and don't want to work in conflict. The goal is to determine the outcome we are trying to achieve by recognizing people and ensuring that our actions align to that intent. It's also important to remember that about 90% of the people in the organization deserve to be recognized often.

Our job as leaders is to develop and coach our teams on what good recognition looks like. The following recommendations will help us do just that. What actions can we take to hardwire recognition in our organization? How can we create a system for recognizing employees?

**First, align recognition to organizational values**. We can use the organization's values to provide specific praise. Also, we can elect to focus on a value a month and recognize people who are doing an exceptional job living the values. At the end of the year, we may give awards to employees who exemplified living the values. That's a great example of blending recognition with rewards.

**Second, recognize people for achieving measurable goals**. We want to know what is expected of us at work. Aligning measurable goals to individual and team expectations helps us know what we are striving to achieve. It's also important to track our progress. Recognize teams and individuals as they make progress toward achieving the goals. Words of recognition keep teams motivated to achieve goals.

**A third way to recognize individuals is celebrating wins and by doing "shout outs" at employee meetings to call out individuals and their positive behaviors.** On our team, we hold weekly team meetings. Prior to that meeting, everyone completes their wins from the prior week. We take time to go around the "zoom room" to share some of the wins on specific weekly contributions. Team members are recognizing each other.

**A fourth way to recognize individuals is by holding relationship building activities like coffees or lunches.** We recognize the employees and build relationships among leaders and employees. When our team comes together several times a year, we end the day with a cookout, enjoying each other's company and having fun. It's something I look forward to – being with people in a friendly, warm and relaxed environment. We have our get togethers in "Frank's Garage." That's my dad's very large garage housed with a kitchen, restroom, dining tables and chairs, and an entertainment system. At one of our get togethers, we forgot that one or our team members was new to our team and had not been to Frank's Garage. When Charleigh was traveling to the get together, she called one of our team members telling them that Frank's Garage did not show up on her GPS. We now make sure we put the address on our agendas!

**A fifth way to recognize people is to include accolades in sections of newsletters, meaningful publications, or appropriate social media channels devoted to recognizing individuals for great work.** We can recognize students, their families, employees, business partners, and friends in the community. Again, we want to be specific about what we are recognizing. Every Monday I host our weekly podcast, *Accelerate Your Performance*. Twice a month I produce episodes on a nine principles tactic. Our Studer Education podcast producers work with our team members to select someone on our team who exemplifies the tactic described on the podcast episode. They post a paragraph on our social media channels, specifically recognizing the team members for being positive examples. The other two weeks of the month, I interview leaders to highlight positive results occurring at our partner organizations. There is so much good to celebrate. Let's do it often.

**A sixth and most important way to express appreciation is to send a hand-written thank you card.** Include specific details of the recognition. If you want to add a special touch, mail it to the home of the individual. Thank you notes are one of the most meaningful ways to appreciate people. Remember, write a note to specifically describe what you appreciate the individual for.

Speaking of Frank's Garage, we had my mom's 80th birthday party in my dad's garage. We organized a party for about 100 people. Following the event, my mom sent me a thank you note that specifically expressed what she appreciated. In one statement on the note, she wrote how much it meant to her that I put a lot of effort into the preparation and hosting of the party even with my busy schedule. I flew in from a week on the road on the late flight on Friday evening before the Saturday party. She is very important to me, so I wanted to put 110% effort into her party even with a busy schedule. Nothing would have gotten in the way of me doing this for her on her 80th birthday. The words expressed in her thank you note made the preparation work for the party worth the time and effort.

**A seventh way to recognize people is to collect the input we receive from rounding sessions with employees.** Remember, one of the key questions is, "Has there been anyone who has been especially helpful to you and what did they do?" Think about how someone would feel if a leader took that specific information and wrote a note to the person being recognized. The leader lets the person receiving the thank you note know who offered the recognition and what was acknowledged as good performance. Who wins? The person receiving the thank you note, the person who recognized the individual, and the leader for sending it. That's a win-win-win!

**Finally, start every meeting by recognizing someone.** As we referenced in the last chapter, put employee recognition as a first item on meeting agendas to start the meeting off with a positive note. Remember recognition connects with organizational values and employee performance. Starting the meeting with employee recognition aligns our conversations to our organizational values.

I've provided several ways to recognize people. You may have some of your own. Recognition goes a long way to showing employees they are valued. Making recognition a habit of practice is one of the most important actions leaders can take to build a strong culture. Why? *What gets recognized, gets repeated*. So, let's make sure we recognize the right things and the right people, and do it often.

## Harvest Wins Every Day

I use the term, "harvest wins" a lot. Not long ago, someone asked me what I meant by that. I thought it was a common term when referencing recognition. So, I searched for the term on the internet. Most of the links connected to harvesting crops. Harvesting is the process of gathering a ripe crop from the fields. Harvesting is the most labor-intensive activity of the growing season.

I know first-hand what it means to harvest. Years ago, when I was a faculty member, I worked different jobs in the summer. At the time, I lived on a 15-acre farm next to my grandfather. He always had an idea. He said, *"Janet – you don't need a job this summer. Let's plant watermelons, harvest them, and sell them on the street corner."* I was excited. We were going into the watermelon business. Well, that excitement lasted until I had to harvest them. A watermelon is heavy and grows on a vine on the ground. My job was to harvest them every day – pick them and put them on the trailer to drive to the corner with our "Watermelons for Sale" sign posted where people could see them. I've never forgotten what it means to harvest something. When I drive down a country road and see "Watermelons for Sale,' I pay my respects to the harvesters.

That's how important harvesting wins is. Harvesting wins means we do the heavy lifting needed to see all the good that we do and contribute to the world. The differences that we make in others' lives are too important to leave on the field. We harvest as many wins as we can every day. We share and celebrate wins all the time. It helps people continue to see that they have purpose, do worthwhile work, and make a difference in the lives of others.

## Chapter 9 Summary

Recognizing and appreciating people must be hardwired in our organizations. Tactics associated with Principle 9 Reward and Recognize Success are critical to apply in all nine principles. It's our last principle because it is one of the most important ones and is connected to the other eight principles.

We depend on our people to achieve organizational excellence. Therefore, we value people for who they are and what they contribute. We value our employees, students, and their families. Great leadership is more important than ever in education. Great leaders know they need a great team to achieve success. Recognizing and appreciating people for what they contribute is a cornerstone to building excellent teams. People want to know what they do matters.

We have the pleasure of working with Dr. Jennifer Lowery, superintendent of the Tea Area School District, South Dakota. The lead Studer Education coach for the school district is Dr. Gayle Juneau-Butler who continuously highlights the specific work being accomplished by Tea Area employees to achieve positive results. Dr. Lowery leads with relentless resolve to create a great school district. She and her district employees apply most of the tactics and tools in *Hardwiring Excellence in Education*. The district employees continuously improve to achieve positive results. Dr. Lowery is never satisfied with good; she is aways striving for the organization to get better and better. She assumes the challenge of leading a best-in-class educational organization.

Both Dr. Lowery and I first started our education careers as mathematics teachers. And both of us have natural tendencies to drive our teams hard while constantly finding the balance for pushing too hard and knowing when to pull back. Both of us moved into leadership positions at a relatively young age. I'm a few decades older than Dr. Lowery. I am amazed at her level of capability early on in her career.

I had an opportunity to interview Dr. Lowery on one of my *Accelerate Your Performance* podcast episodes. The interview was about what it takes to be a great leader and what that meant to her as the superintendent of Tea Area School District. Dr. Lowery spoke about how important it is for her to recognize her team for what they are accomplishing. She talks about how fortunate she has been to be where she is and how she wants to give back to others. Without a doubt, Dr. Lowery continues to drive her team to be one of the best school systems in the country. She wouldn't settle for anything less. All the while, she understands how Principle 9 is key to supporting and mentoring new leaders in our education profession.

One of the things I've learned about recognition is that we don't have to worry about limiting it. We don't have to worry if there's enough to go around. The more we recognize people, the more people will recognize others. We all want our good work to be applauded. We also want to be appreciated for our inherent value as a colleague and a human being. Principle 9 is the last principle and one that is connected to all others. That's why we end with this principle – it's part of everything we do to build a place where people want to do the deep work to move an organization from good to great and great to greater.

# CONCLUSION

In 2003, Quint Studer wrote a book that chronicled his personal story and described ways to apply the nine principles initially focused on the healthcare profession. The book was called *Hardwiring Excellence: Purpose, Worthwhile Work, Making a Difference*. At the time, a company he started, Studer Group, was working with healthcare organizations to create and sustain world-class organizations. As I've mentioned, I learned about the work being done in healthcare and had an opportunity to join Studer Group in 2010 to prepare for a full launch of a new division, Studer Education, which I've had the pleasure of serving as the founder and leader of a growing and evolving team.

Throughout the past decade, I've been in the field with educational leaders discovering how to apply evidence-based practices to make the greatest impact in education. We've done so by evolving the Nine Principles Framework and the associated tools and tactics for each principle. During this journey, we've had an opportunity to join a larger organization, Huron Consulting, dedicated to helping us make a greater impact in our education profession. I am fortunate to work with Huron executive leaders, Mark Hussey (CEO) and Curt Whelan (Managing Director of Strategic Growth), who believe in me, our team, and our work.

I am fortunate to be joined by a talented and thoughtful Studer Education team highly committed to providing the greatest service to each other and those we serve every day. I am most fortunate to work alongside the best educational leaders in the country who are committed to excellence and to developing their people to apply the tools and tactics described in this book. We intentionally call the organizations we work with *partners* because together we are improving the leadership skills of our teams to be at their best. We all chose the education profession to be of service to others. I am grateful to leaders who partner with us to assume this awesome responsibility.

I close this book by telling a story of how interconnected we are in this world and why this book is important to build positive momentum in our profession that is sustainable over time. In the conclusion section of Quint's 2003 book, he concludes with Brian's Story.

As Quint traveled the country talking to healthcare leaders, he always carried a baseball cap from the University of Illinois Chicago (UIC) in his briefcase. There is a picture of a flame on the cap. The cap belonged to his nephew, Brian Fitzpatrick, who played on a baseball scholarship for the UIC Flames. December 1995, Brian took a trip with the team to Australia. On his return, his dad, and his older brother, Mike Jr., picked him up from the airport. Brian was enthusiastic about sharing all his stories from his trip with his mom, Kathy, so they went back to the Fitzpatrick home. Then he hopped in the car to go visit his high school buddies. Afterwards, he stopped by Mike Jr.'s home to talk some more and fell asleep on Mike

Jr.'s couch. At 5:00 the next morning, on Christmas Eve, Brian woke up, got in his car, and started to drive home. But he never made it. Brian was killed in a car accident that Christmas Eve morning. At Brian's wake, the entire UIC baseball team walked in wearing their uniforms and lined up along the casket to honor Brian. Brian's high school baseball cap and the UIC baseball cap from his first win as Division 1 college pitcher were placed with Brian in the casket.

I've heard Quint talk about Brian carrying a flame because of the difference he made with others. Brian played baseball for a college called the UIC Flames. Quint expresses that Brian's flame had been extinguished on this earth much earlier than anyone would have imagined. During Quint's presentations, he asks people to leave with a little of Brian's flame to keep their passion ignited for the work they do and to spread good energy to others.

The roots of Studer Education are part of Brian's Story. The flame is a meaningful symbol to our organization. The people we work with carry a flame that continues to burn and spread to others. Good people find each other – that's what keeps the flame burning bright.

We honor our work with a flame. We have small pins that are in the shape of a flame that we give to others encouraging them to keep their flame burning brightly by applying the tools and tactics described in this book. Our Difference-Maker Award is in the shape of a beautiful flame. It's our way of honoring leaders who are keeping the flame of their organizations burning bright. And now, almost 30 years after Brian's death, my colleague (Dr. Gayle Juneau-Butler) and I have the honor of working with several University of Illinois Chicago (UIC) leaders in applying the Nine Principles Framework. It's a small, powerfully interconnected world.

The Nine Principles Framework operated by the Organizational Flywheel makes us better leaders and better people, always knowing that we can improve to get better at our craft. Our actions and behaviors as leaders affect the well-being of students, their families, and our employees. We focus on both the emotional and rational aspects of our organizations by building inspiring workplaces, strengthening our people, and accelerating results. The interconnectedness of the nine principles ignites the flame that spins the flywheel faster and faster.

Since the inception of Studer Education in 2010, I have been honored to work with our Studer Education team and partners we serve in what has become a national learning laboratory with thousands of educators who strive every day to make a difference in the lives of others. I express my gratitude to all of you who took time to read *Hardwiring Excellence in Education*. I hope the tools and tactics associated with the Nine Principles Framework help you spin your organizational flywheel.

At the end of the day, let's ask ourselves – Did we lead in ways for people to have purpose, do worthwhile work, and make a difference? When we do, we hardwire excellence in education and keep the flame burning.

# ACKNOWLEDGMENTS

I am deeply appreciative of people who have contributed to the body of work that has enhanced and advanced the Nine Principles Framework. My colleagues in healthcare started a journey that contributed to making healthcare organizations a great place for employees to work and patients to receive care. That work continues to be more important than ever. I have the utmost appreciation for our dedicated healthcare workers who are saving lives every day.

My initial connection with healthcare coaches and professionals and the introduction by Dr. Pat Greco to the body of work on continuous improvement at the Carnegie Foundation for the Advancement of Teaching influence the continued development of the Nine Principles Framework.

As I think back on the beginning of Studer Education, I extend my deepest appreciation to Dr. Robin Largue. Two decades ago, while at the University of West Florida we co-created TeacherReady, a world-wide online alternative teacher certification program. We committed to providing an excellent program to individuals who had a passion to teach but were not credentialed. I started my K12 teaching career as an alternatively certified teacher. I knew there were people like me who awoke every day wanting to teach. Robin's experience as a high school teacher and principal, a senior leader in a school district, and a director of UWF's educational leadership program contributed to building what we believe is one of the best teacher preparation programs in the world.

As I started Studer Education, working with UWF, we created an agreement where the two of us could continue the program as part of Studer Education in partnership with UWF. As we continued to grow the program, we shifted some of the responsibility to a TeacherReady team that gave Robin and I a chance to engage with school districts to refine and apply the Nine Principles Framework. We started with one district at a time, serving as the only two coaches and leaders to grow our organization. And, that we did. Today, we are serving about 120 school districts a year. We also enroll about 1000 students a year in our TeacherReady program. I was the founder of Studer Education, but the organization would not be where it is today without the first decade of leadership Robin provided to our team. Robin retired from our organization in March of 2022 knowing that she helped create a solid foundation for our Studer Education leaders to take our organization into the next decade of service to our partners and students. Today, we have a senior leadership team that will indeed take our organization to the next level. Robin, thank you for working in partnership with me to advance the Nine Principles Framework over the years that serve as the guiding principles for Studer Education.

I recognize some very special colleagues who have helped me make this book a reality.

- Thank you, Dr. KK Owen. You are a wealth of information that I relied on. When I asked you a question or for needed information, within 24 hours it was sent to my inbox. Also, you are a great teacher of the tools and tactics associated with the Nine Principles Framework.

- Thank you, Mandy Gagliardi. You know I have something in my mind, and you are always trying to figure it out and aren't satisfied until you do. Thank you for designing the book cover and helping with the graphics and layout to get the look and feel just right.
- Thank you, Dr. Theresa Vernetson. You've been the person I could turn to for guidance and advice most of my professional life. Your continued review and editing of the book is invaluable. You've made me a better writer over the years and I'm still learning.
- Thank you, Deborah McIntyre. When I needed encouragement, you gave it. When I needed help managing my schedule and time to make this book a reality, you made it happen. When I needed kindness, you gave it. You are an invaluable member of our team and to me.
- Thank you, Dr. Julie Kunselman and Dr. Pat Greco for helping me with the Bibliography that supports each of the principles. You all are always resourceful and quick to respond and contribute.
- Thank you, Dr. Melissa Matarazzo. You are the glue that holds our team together. You are quick to help me balance my priorities that help our team and me. That's been more important than ever this past year.
- Thank you, Dr. Sarah Miller. You always step up to the plate to help. When difficulties arise or something feels impossible, you build strength in our team and me, and we needed that this last year.

One of the highlights of my work is having the privilege of leading our Studer Education team. To our team - You demonstrate care and concern for each other and our "customers." I am so proud of the work we all do together. I couldn't write this book in good faith unless you all practice the nine principles. That's what we expect of each other. Thank you for making me a better leader and person.

After three decades of being a working professional, I am more inspired than I've ever been because of the leaders we get to work with around the country. As a coach working with my other Studer coach colleagues, I feel indebted to the executives and leaders for giving us the opportunity to work with them and their organizations. I say it time and again, I feel like the leaders we partner with become our life-long friends. We are all doing the right work to revolutionize the education profession. I'm excited to continue to partner with our current partners on this important journey and look forward to partnering with leaders who want to join.

Finally, I am deeply indebted to the value the leaders highlighted in this book give to my life. You give me purpose, make my work worthwhile, and make a difference in my life as well as the lives you touch every day. Thank you.

# ABOUT THE AUTHOR

Janet is the founder of Studer Education, and a managing director for Huron Consulting Group. She has an extensive background advising educational institutions on strategic planning, leadership development, workplace culture, and operational improvement. Janet leads a team to apply the Nine Principles Framework described in *Hardwiring Excellence in Education* to support leaders to achieve organizational excellence.

Before starting Studer Education, Janet spent nearly 20 years at the University of West Florida (UWF) as a professor and dean of the College of Professional Studies. She initiated an institute to serve PK-20 and community organizations. She received and oversaw $17 million of grant and contract projects and achieved one of UWF's research distinction awards. While at UWF, Janet co-created an online teacher certification program that prepares second-career teachers worldwide that she continues to lead today.

Janet transitioned from higher education to work with the founder of Studer Group, Quint Studer, to determine how best to transfer leadership best practices in healthcare to education. With this transition, she built Studer Education to a growing organization serving organizational leaders to be at their best to achieve high performing results.

Janet is the author of several books that focus on leadership excellence and continuous improvement. She has a B.S. in business from Florida State University; an M.Ed. in Educational Leadership from the University of West Florida; and a Ph.D. in Measurement and Evaluation from Florida State University.

# BIBLIOGRAPHY ALIGNED TO THE NINE PRINCIPLES FRAMEWORK

## Chapter 1 Principle 1: Commit to Excellence


Ashkenas, R. (2009). *Simply Effective: How to Cut Through Complexity in Your Organization and Get Things Done.* Harvard Business Review Press.

Bryk, A. S. (2020). *Improvement in Action: Advancing Quality in America's Schools.* Harvard Education Press.

Collins, J., & Lazier, W. (2020). *BE 2.0 (Beyond Entrepreneurship 2.0): Turning Your Business Into an Enduring Great Company.* Penguin Publishing Group.

Collins, J. (2001). *Good to Great: Why Some Companies Make the Leap ... and Others Don't.* Random House Business.

Collins, J. (2001, January 1). Level 5 Leadership: The triumph of humility and fierce resolve. *Harvard Business Review.* https://hbr.org/2001/01/level-5-leadership-the-triumph-of-humility-and-fierce-resolve-2

Deming, W. E. (1986). *Out of the Crisis.* Cambridge University Press.

Feinbloom, D. (2008). *The triple aim and the future of quality improvement.* Retrieved December 4, 2022, from https://www.medscape.org/viewarticle/578138

Greco, P. (2019). Healing our systems and making improvement stick. *School Administrator Magazine, 76*(3), 14-20.

Haidt, J. (2006). *The Happiness Hypothesis: Finding Modern Truth in Ancient Wisdom.* Basic Books.

Heath, C., & Heath, D. (2010). *Switch: How to Change Things When Change Is Hard.* Crown.

Kotter, J. P., Akhtar, V., & Gupta, G. (2021). *Change: How Organizations Achieve Hard-to-Imagine Results in Uncertain and Volatile Times.* Wiley.

Langley, G. J., Norman, C. L., Nolan, K. M., Nolan, T. W., Moen, R. D., & Provost, L. P. (2009). *The Improvement Guide: A Practical Approach to Enhancing Organizational Performance.* Wiley.

Lencioni, P. (2020). *The Motive: Why So Many Leaders Abdicate Their Most Important Responsibilities.* Wiley.

Park, S., & Takahashi, S. (2013, October). *90-Day Cycle Handbook*. Carnegie Foundation for the Advancement of Teaching and Learning. https://www.carnegiefoundation.org/wp-content/uploads/2014/09/90DC_Handbook_external_10_8.pdf

Senge, P. M., Cambron-McCabe, N., Lucas, T., Smith, B., Dutton, J., & Kleiner, A. (2012). *Schools That Learn (Updated and Revised): A Fifth Discipline Fieldbook for Educators, Parents, and Everyone Who Cares About Education.* Crown.

## Chapter 2 Principle 2: Measures that Matter

Ashmore, S., & Runyan, K. (2014). *Introduction to Agile Methods.* Addison-Wesley.

Blochowiak, C. (2021). *The positive deviance improvement approach in education: A case study of school and district application*. [Doctoral dissertation, University of Wisconsin – Madison].

Covey, S. R. (2004). *7 Habits of Highly Effective People.* Free Press.

Creighton, S. (2022, May 26). *William E. Deming: The master of continual improvement of quality.* Retrieved December 4, 2022, from https://blog.lifeqisystem.com/william-edwards-deming

Deming, E. (1986). *Plan-Do-Study-Act (PDSA) Cycle: The Key to organizational learning.* https://deming.org/explore/pdsa/

Gawande, A. (2010). *The Checklist Manifesto: How to Get Things Right.* Henry Holt and Company.

Greco, P. (2021). Learning from wicked challenges. *School Administrator Magazine, 78*(4), 26-30.

Hamilton, A., Reeves, D. B., Clinton, J. M., & Hattie, J. (2022). *Building to Impact: The 5D Implementation Playbook for Educators.* SAGE Publications.

Koch, R. (2017). *The 80/20 Principle: The Secret of Achieving More with Less.* Nicholas Brealey Publishing.

LeMahieu, P. G., Nordstrum, L. E., & Gale, D. (2017). Positive deviance: learning from positive anomalies. *Quality Assurance in Education*, *25*(1), 109-124. https://doi.org/10.1108/QAE-12-2016-0083

Niven, P. R. (2008). *Balanced Scorecard: Step-by-Step for Government and Nonprofit Agencies.* Wiley.

Peurach, D. J., Russell, J. L., Cohen-Vogel, L., & Penuel, W. (Eds.) (2022). *The Foundational Handbook on Improvement Research in Education.* Rowman & Littlefield Publishers.

Sherer, D., Norman J., Bryk A., Peurach, D., Vasudeva A., & McMahon K. (2020, February). *Evidence for improvement: An integrated analytic approach for supporting networks in education*. The Carnegie Foundation for the Advancement of Teaching. https://files.eric.ed.gov/fulltext/ED606554.pdf

## Chapter 3 Principle 3 Build a Culture Around Service

Anderson, J. (2013). *Principle-Based Leadership: Driving Your Success as a Leader*. iUniverse.

Blake, R. R., & Mouton, J. S. (1982). Theory and research for developing a science of leadership. *The Journal of Applied Behavioral Science, 18*(3), 275–291. https://doi.org/10.1177/002188638201800304

Collins, J. (2000, June). *Aligning action and values*. The Forum. https://www.jimcollins.com/article_topics/articles/aligning-action.html.

Grant, H. M., Crutchfield, L. R. (2012). *Forces for Good: The Six Practices of High-Impact Nonprofits.* Wiley.

Hui, B., Ng, J., Berzaghi, E., Cunningham-Amos, L., & Kogan, A. (2020), Rewards of kindness: A meta-analysis of the link between prosociality and well-being. *Psychological Bulletin, 146*(12), 1084-1116. https://www.apa.org/pubs/journals/releases/bul-bul0000298.pdf

Reichheld, F., Darnell, D., & Burns, M. (2021). *Winning on Purpose: The Unbeatable Strategy of Loving Customers.* Harvard Business Review Press.

Reichheld, F., & Markey, R. (2011). *The Ultimate Question 2.0: How Net Promoter Companies Thrive in a Customer-driven World.* Harvard Business Review Press.

Sherman, V. C. (1993). *Creating the New American Hospital: A Time for Greatness.* Jossey-Bass.

## Chapter 4: Principle 4 Develop People to Develop People

Argote, L. (2012). *Organizational Learning: Creating, Retaining and Transferring Knowledge.* Springer.

Baker, E. M. (2016). *The Symphony of Profound Knowledge: W. Edwards Deming's Score for Leading, Performing, and Living in Concert.* iUniverse.

Brown, B. (2018). *Dare to Lead: Brave Work, Tough Conversations, Whole Hearts.* Random House.

Dixon, C., & Palmer, S. (2020, March). *Transforming educational systems toward continuous improvement: A reflection guide for K-12 executive leaders.* Carnegie Foundation for the Advancement of Teaching and Learning. https://www.carnegiefoundation.org/wp-content/uploads/2020/04/Carnegie_Transform_EdSystems.pdf

Grissom, J., Egalite, A., & Lindsay, C. (2021, February). *How principals affect students and schools: A systematic synthesis of two decades of research.* Wallace Foundation. https://www.wallacefoundation.org/knowledge-center/Documents/How-Principals-Affect-Students-and-Schools.pdf

Harrell, E. (2016). Succession planning: What the research says. *Harvard Business Review, 12,* 70-74.

Higgins, M., Ishimaru, A., Holcombe, R., & Fowler, A. (2011). Examining organizational learning in schools: The role of psychological safety, experimentation, and leadership that reinforces learning. *Journal of Educational Change, 13*(1), 1-28.

Learning Policy Institute. (2017, September 13). *What's the cost of teacher turnover.* https://learningpolicyinstitute.org/product/the-cost-of-teacher-turnover

Maxwell, J. (2013). *The 5 Levels of Leadership: Proven Steps to Maximize Your Potential.* Center Street.

Senge, P. M., Lucas, T., Dutton, J., Cambron-McCabe, N., & Smith, B. (2012). *Schools That Learn (Updated and Revised): A Fifth Discipline Fieldbook for Educators, Parents, and Everyone Who Cares About Education.* Crown.

Sibisi S., & Kappers, G. (2022, April 5). Onboarding can make or break a new hire's experience. *Harvard Business Review.*

https://hbr.org/2022/04/onboarding-can-make-or-break-a-new-hires-experience

Speck, M., & Knipe, C. (Eds.) (2005). *Why Can't We Get It Right? Designing High-Quality Professional Development for Standards-Based Schools.* Corwin.

Stevenson, L., & Mills, B. (2022, November 15). *The Features of Effective School Groups: Measuring workforce sustainability of effective school groups.* Education Policy Institute. https://epi.org.uk/wp-content/uploads/2022/11/Measuring-Workforce-Sustainability-of-Effective-School-Groups-2022-1.pdf

Studer, Q. (2003). *Hardwiring Excellence. Purpose, Worthwhile Work, and Making a Difference.* Fire Starter Publishing.

The New Teacher Project. (2012, July 30). *The Irreplaceables: Understanding the Real Retention Crisis in America's Urban Schools.* https://tntp.org/assets/documents/TNTP_Irreplaceables_2012.pdf

## Chapter 5 Principle 5 Focus on Employee Engagement

Ahlstrom, J. (2014). *How to Succeed with Continuous Improvement: A Primer for Becoming the Best in the World.* McGraw-Hill Education.

American Psychological Association. (2021). *The American workforce faces compounding pressure: APA's 2021 Work and well-being survey results*. https://www.apa.org/pubs/reports/work-well-being/compounding-pressure-2021

Caproni, P. J. (2016). *The Science of Success: What Researchers Know that You Should Know.* Van Rye Publishing, LLC.

Finnegan, R. P. (2018). *The Power of Stay Interviews for Engagement and Retention.* Society for Human Resource Management.

Jobvite. (2022). *Job seeker nation report: Dynamic motivations of modern workers.* https://www.jobvite.com/lp/2022-job-seeker-nation-report/

Keller, S., & Meaney, M. (2017). *Leading Organizations: Ten Timeless Truths.* Bloomsbury.

Kruse, K. (2012, September 4). Why employee engagement? These 28 research studies prove the benefits. *Forbes*. Retrieved December 4, 2022, from https://www.forbes.com/sites/kevinkruse/2012/09/04/why-employee-engagement

Lencioni, P. (2012). *The Advantage: Why Organizational Health Trumps Everything Else In Business.* Wiley.

Owens, B. P., Baker, W. E., Sumpter, D. M., & Cameron, K. S. (2016). Relational energy at work: Implications for job engagement and job performance. *Journal of Applied Psychology, 101*(1), 35-49. https://doi.org/10.1037/apl0000032

Pilcher, J. (2019). Tools and tactics of organizational excellence: The work of creating a high-performing school system through continuous improvement. *School Administrator Magazine, 76*(3), 28-31.

Pilcher, J., & Largue, R. (2009). *How to lead teachers to become great: It's all about student learning.* Fire Starter Publishing.

Society for Human Resource Management. (2016). *Society for human resource management research overview: Employee engagement.* https://www.shrm.org/hr-today/trends-and-forecasting/special-reports-and-expert-views/Documents/Research%20Overview%20Employee%20Engagement.pdf

Studer, Q. & Pilcher, J. (2015). *Maximize Performance: Creating a Culture for Educational Excellence.* Fire Starter Publishing.

Zãrraga Oberty, C., & Bonache Perez, J. (2003). Assessing the team environment for knowledge sharing: An empirical analysis. *The International Journal of Human Resource Management, 14*(7), 1227-1245.

## Chapter 6 Principle 6 Be Accountable

Amabile, T., & Kramer, S. (2011). The Power of small wins. *Harvard Business Review.* https://hbr.org/2011/05/the-power-of-small-wins

Dennis, P. (2006). *Getting the Right Things Done: A Leader's Guide to Planning and Execution.* Lean Enterprise Institute.

Friedman, R. (2021, October 21). 5 things high performing teams do differently. *Harvard Business Review.* https://hbr.org/2021/10/5-things-high-performing-teams-do-differently

Heifetz, R., Grashow, A., & Linsky, M. (2009). *The Practice of Adaptive Leadership: Tools and Tactics for Changing Your Organization and the World.* Harvard Business Press.

Jobvite. (2022). *Job seeker nation report: Dynamic motivations of modern workers.* https://www.jobvite.com/lp/2022-job-seeker-nation-report/

Lencioni, P. (2002). *The 5 Dysfunctions of Team: A Leadership Fable.* Jossey-Bass.

Linkner, J. (2021). *Big Little Breakthroughs: How Small, Everyday Innovations Drive Oversized Results.* Post Hill Press.

McChesney, C., Covey, S., & Huling, J. (2012). *The 4 Disciplines of Execution: Achieving Your Wildly Important Goals.* Simon & Schuster.

Molinaro, V. (2020). *Accountable Leaders: Inspire a Culture Where Everyone Steps Up, Takes Ownership, and Delivers Results.* Wiley.

Molinaro, V. (2017). *The leadership accountability gap: A global study exploring the real state in organizations today.*

Lee Hecht Harrison. https://www.lhh.com/lhhpenna/en/-/media/lhh/uk/pdfs/lhh-leadership-accountability-global-research-report.pdf

Porath, C. & Pearson, C. (2012, January – February). The Price of Incivility. *Harvard Business Review*, https://hbr.org/2013/01/the-price-of-incivility

Scholtes, P. R. (1997). *The Leader's Handbook: Making Things Happen, Getting Things Done.* McGraw-Hill Education.

Shook, J. (2008). *Managing to Learn: Using the A3 Management Process to Solve Problems, Gain Agreement, Mentor and Lead.* Lean Enterprise Institute.

Studer, Q. (2008). *Results That Last: Hardwiring Behaviors That Will Take Your Company to the Top.* Wiley.

Sullivan, D., & Hardy, D. B. (2020). *Who Not How: The Formula to Achieve Bigger Goals Through Accelerating Teamwork.* Hay House.

## Chapter 7 Principle 7 Align Behaviors to Goals and Values

Carpenter, R. (2021). Building resilience in an organization. *School Administrator Magazine, 78*(4), 31-34.

Dorkenoo, C., Nyarko I., Semordey, E., & Agbemava, E. (2022). The concept of workplace values and its effect on employee performance. *International Journal of Asian Academic Research Social Sciences & Humanities, 2,* 287-300.

Edmondson, A. C. (2018). *The Fearless Organization: Creating Psychological Safety in the Workplace for Learning, Innovation, and Growth.* Wiley.

Heifetz, R., Linsky, M., & Grashow, A. (2009). *The Practice of Adaptive Leadership: Tools and Tactics for Changing Your Organization and the World.* Harvard Business Press.

Kotter, J. (2008). *A Sense of Urgency.* Harvard Business Press.

Pilcher, J., & Largue, R. (2021). Rethinking how we design programs: Listening to our students. In P. Northrup, K. Rasmussen, & R. Colson (Eds.), *Career Ready Education Through Experiential Learning*. IGI Global Publisher.

Scholtes, P. R., Joiner, B. L., & Streibel, B. J. (2003). *The Team Handbook.* Oriel.

Senge, P. M. (2006). *The Fifth Discipline: The Art and Practice of the Learning Organization.* Random House Business Books.

Sinek, S. (2009). *Start with Why: How Great Leaders Inspire Everyone to Take Action.* Portfolio.

Starbird, D., & Cavanagh, R. (2010). *Building Engaged Team Performance: Align Your Processes and People to Achieve Game-Changing Business Results.* McGraw Hill.

Sternke, J. (2019). Cascading communication. *School Administrator Magazine, 76*(3), 25-27.

Toussaint, J., Gerard, R., & Adams, E. (2010). *On the Mend: Revolutionizing Healthcare to Save Lives and Transform the Industry.* Lean Enterprise Institute.

Weick, K. E. (1984). Small wins: Redefining the scale of social problems. *American Psychologist, 39*(1), 40-49.

Weick, K. E., & Sutcliffe, K. M. (2015). *Managing the Unexpected: Sustained Performance in a Complex World.* Wiley.

## Chapter 8 Principle 8 Communicate at All Levels

Adu-Oppong, A. (2014). Communication in the workplace: Guidelines for improving effectiveness. *Global Journal of Commerce & Management Perspective, 3*(5), 208-213.

Bodell, L. (2016). *Why Simple Wins: Escape the Complexity Trap and Get To Work That Matters.* Taylor & Francis.

*Bucăța,* G., & Rizescu M., (2017). The role of communication in enhancing work effectiveness of an organization. *Land*

*Forces Academy Review, 22.* http://dx.doi.org/10.1515/raft-2017-0008
Carucci, R. (2015, December 9). Why it matters that your people know they matter. *Forbes.* Retrieved December 4, 2022, from https://www.forbes.com/sites/roncarucci/2015/12/09/why-it-matters-your-people-know-they-matter
Clifton, J., & Harter J. (2021). *Wellbeing at Work.* Gallup Press.
Covey, S. M. (2008). *The Speed of Trust: The One Thing that Changes Everything.* Simon & Schuster.
Lowery, J. (2021). Decision making that sustains people and builds relationships. *School Administrator Magazine, 78*(4), 35-37.
Sinek, S. (2009). *Start with Why: How Great Leaders Inspire Everyone to Take Action.* Portfolio.

## Chapter 9 Principle 9 Reward and Recognize Success

Bloch, S. (2000). Positive deviants and their power on transformational leadership. *Journal of Change Management, 1*(3), 273-279.
Brown, J., & Wong, J. (2017, June 6). How gratitude changes you and your brain. *Greater Good Magazine: Science-Based Insights for a Meaningful Life*. Retrieved December 4, 2022, from https://greatergood.berkeley.edu/article/item/how_gratitude_changes_you_and_your_brain
Burke, W. W. (2017). *Organization Change: Theory and Practice.* SAGE Publications.
Folkman, J. (2017, May 18). According to research, here's the single key to improving employee engagement. *Forbes.* Retrieved December 4, 2022, from https://www.forbes.com/sites/joefolkman/2017/05/18/according-to-research-heres-the-single-key-to-improving-employee-engagement

Kaye, B., & Jordan-Evans, S. (2013). *10 things you can offer your employees that are Better than a Raise*. Berrett-Koehler Publishers. https://ideas.bkconnection.com/download-10-things-that-you-can-offer-your-employees-that-are-better-than-a-raise

O'Flaherty S., Sanders M., & Whillans A. (2021, March 29). Research: A Little Recognition Can Provide a Big Morale Boost. *Harvard Business Review*. https://hbr.org/2021/03/research-a-little-recognition-can-provide-a-big-morale-boost

Robbins, M. (2019, November 12). Why employees need both recognition and appreciation. *Harvard Business Review.* https://hbr.org/2019/11/why-employees-need-both-recognition-and-appreciation

Stoerkel, E. (2019, February 4). The science and research on gratitude and happiness. *Positive Psychology.* Retrieved December 4, 2022, from https://positivepsychology.com/gratitude-happiness-research/